# LEFTY'S LITTLE LIBRARY OF FLY FISHING

LEFTY'S LITTLE LIBRARY OF FLY FISHING

# THE TEENY TECHNIQUE FOR STEELHEAD AND SALMON

*Good Fishing*
*Jim Teeny*

**JIM TEENY**

**ODYSSEUS EDITIONS**

*Birmingham, Alabama*

THE TEENY TECHNIQUE FOR STEELHEAD
AND SALMON

Published by Odysseus Editions, Inc. under the direction of:

Leslie B. Adams, President & Publisher

Bernard "Lefty" Kreh, Editor-in-Chief

Amanda P. Adams, Vice President

Elizabeth Davis, Administration

John Randolph, Editorial Consultant

Robin McDonald, Designer

FRONTISPIECE: *Jim Teeny with a beautiful steelhead on the Kispiox River in British Columbia.*

# CONTENTS

OVERLEAF: *Steve Dorn fishing a prime steelhead stream located south of Ketchikan, Alaska.*

# LEFTY'S PREFACE

He may be "teeny" in height and name, but he is a giant among fly fishermen. Jim Teeny is a natural-born fisherman. Many anglers work hard and finally master much of the sport. Others, very few others, have an intuitive nature. Jim is the kind of fisherman who may have never been to a region, and certainly for a very brief time may not do well, but in a short time, I guarantee you that he will become one of the top anglers in the area.

I have said many times that I rate Jim Teeny among the best natural fishermen that I have had the pleasure of fishing with. He would have made a helluva cave man — his family would have never gone hungry.

I've stalked many streams with Jim, and he is the closest thing I've seen to a great blue heron closing in on its meal — an unsuspecting fish. In fact, Jim becomes so intent on pursuing fish that I think there are times if someone goosed him, he would leap right into the river!

But Jim is more than a good angler, he is one of those rare anglers who is innovative. And, like anyone who breaks with tradition and discovers new and better ways to do something, his technique has been criticized by those who are, perhaps, not as creative or bold enough to expand their horizons beyond the comfortable but rigid boundaries of tradition.

This is not unusual in fly fishing. A classic example is when Scientific Anglers made the first sinking line at the insistence of a number of fly-fishing professionals, including myself. There were, however, some in the profession who had always fished a floating line and declared that using a sinking line was not really true fly fishing. Moreover, these people declared that its use was unethical since it was taking unfair advantage of the fish.

Another example: When tarpon fishing started to become popular, some anglers who had always used a basic tapered leader — with the weakest section (the tippet) attached to the fly — declared that using a heavy bite leader between the fly and the tippet was unethical, despite the fact that they were losing so many fish when their light tippets were being severed by the abrasive mouth of the tarpon.

Or, when I first advised using lead eyes on fly patterns, some people wrote to magazine editors declaring that using lead eyes was the same as using jigs.

Or, some trout fishermen will aggressively insist that it is unethical to use chum as an aid to tease fish into taking a fly. Yet, these same people will maintain careful records in order to be on the stream when a hatch occurs. Apparently it never dawns on them that they are being assisted in a similar way by the natural chum that Mother Nature provides.

Fortunately for our sport, all of the examples mentioned here, plus many other techniques that were once regarded as being radical departures from tradition, have long since become accepted — and enjoyed — by most fly fishermen.

The subject of this book — Jim's technique for fly fishing to the steelhead and Pacific salmon that inhabit his home waters of the Pacific Northwest — is similarly controversial to some anglers. It may be to you. You'll just have to make your own decision about that. But whether you adopt Jim's techniques or not, I guarantee it's worth learning them to see how a true master adapts and changes traditional technique to accomplish his purpose.

When I started the Library, I established the basic principle that every book in it — either those written by me or those written under commission from me by other fly-fishing professionals whose work I admire — would attempt to provide our readers with the very best information and the most effective fly-fishing techniques that have been developed. It was then, and remains my hope now, that this would help our readers improve their individual fly-fishing skills, increase their enjoyment of the sport, and consequently (and certainly most importantly) *catch more fish* in an ethical manner as the sport demands.

Jim's technique on steelhead and salmon certainly comes up to that standard, as far as I am concerned. While Jim knows how and understands how to use all the traditional dry and wet-fly techniques, his method of locating fish and presenting flies to them in the water column where they are holding *is the most deadly method I've ever seen in all my years of fly fishing for steelhead and Pacific salmon.* I recommend it to you.

Of course, I recognize that most of us would, most of the time, prefer to catch our steelhead and salmon on the surface. The trouble is that weather and water conditions for doing this don't always exist. But after you have read this book, if you choose to adopt Jim's technique, you will catch more steelhead and Pacific salmon than you ever did before, at all times of the year and under all types of conditions. Of that I can assure you.

Tight lines — but not too tight!

Lefty Kreh
Hunt Valley, Maryland

OVERLEAF: *Jim Teeny fishing for spring chinook salmon on the Wind River, Washington.*

# INTRODUCTION

Since I was old enough to hold a fly rod in my hands, I have been fishing for steelhead and all species of Pacific salmon, both in my native waters of the Pacific Northwest of the United States, as well as throughout British Columbia and Alaska. So, although in this book I will also make mention of the steelhead and salmon fisheries of the upper midwestern and eastern United States, it is in the Pacific Northwest where I learned what I know about fly fishing to these species, so most of my references will be to my home waters. I confess I have not done much steelhead and salmon fishing outside the Pacific Northwest. Why go across the country to fish when I've got the best there is in my backyard? But I have been told by a number of steelhead and salmon anglers that my techniques will travel and work well on migratory steelhead and salmon anywhere in the world.

Also, for the balance of this book, unless I indicate otherwise, what I have to say applies to both steelhead as well as the five species of Pacific salmon, because the behavioral characteristics of these fish, and the way I advocate fly fishing for them, are similar enough, as far as I am concerned, to not require much distinction.

I have tried all the various techniques that have been developed over the years for presenting dry flies on the surface or wet flies just under the surface. And I am the first to admit that under the right conditions, including the season of the year, the air and water temperature, the water clarity, the holding position of the fish, etc., surface or just-under-the-surface dry or wet-fly presentations to steelhead and salmon can be very effective and exciting. And when conditions are right, it's just great. Having a fish with a head the size of a football suddenly rise from the water and snatch your fly from the surface film is an awesome fly-fishing experience!

But on how many of your fishing days do you encounter ideal conditions? I know that in my neck of the woods, while I am always bragging to outsiders about our great weather in the Pacific Northwest, I have to confess that we don't see many days when conditions could be described as ideal.

I have never done much dry-fly fishing for steelhead, simply because I started fishing wet flies as a kid, and then, after I developed my Teeny Nymph series of fly patterns, I figured that if there was a product on the market with my name on it, it just wouldn't be right for me to be fishing anything else.

But since it's my favorite sport, I've studied all the techniques on steelhead and salmon fishing, mostly by observing other top steelhead anglers and reading their books. We are fortunate that there are a number of excellent general steelhead and salmon fly-fishing books on the market, many of which include detailed instructions on any number of dry-fly techniques that are in use today, chief among them waking and skating. So, even though waking and skating a dry fly are not part of my technique, for those of you who are not familiar with them, I'll give you a brief definition.

*Waking* and *skating* describe similar techniques for imparting a special action or motion to a floating dry fly. Typically, after a down-and-across cast the angler will make an initial mend in the fly line, and then hold his rod in a position that will impart sufficient tension to the line to force the fly to move across the surface of the water. "Skating" generally applies to the use of a heavily hackled dry fly, such as a big Humpy or Wulff or Bomber, that will ride or "skate" along the top of the water without drowning. "Waking" a fly, which is accomplished with more or less the same type of line manipulation, generally applies to dry flies which are designed so that under tension they will either plow just under, or half under, the surface of the water, or sink slightly and then bob back up. In either case this means imprinting a wake — "waking" — on the surface behind the fly to attract fish. Typical waking patterns are a Waller Waker or a Bubblehead.

Many books also discuss in detail various surface wet-fly techniques, such as use of the greased line and the riffling hitch. Here's how I define them.

*Greased line* is a wet-fly technique reportedly developed by Arthur A.E. Wood, a British Atlantic salmon angler, and later described in the fly-fishing classic, *Greased Line Fishing for Salmon* (1935) by "Jock Scott" (Donald Rudd). Wood discovered that if he dressed (greased) his fly line with fat from a red stag, the grease would serve to add additional floatation to his line, eliminating or substantially reducing its drag in the water. In this manner, he could suspend his fly just under the surface of the water and control its path with manipulation of his rod tip. He could either speed up or slow down the swing of the fly, in order to lead the fly in a desired target direction, or with a series of up or downstream mends he could create numerous drag-free floats. This is a very useful technique, and is widely employed today by wet-fly fishermen who can now substitute Wood's red stag fat (which is sort of hard to come by at most fly-fishing shops these days) with any number of modern silicone dressings.

I have occasionally greased-line fished with my Teeny nymph and leech patterns, and it can be a very successful way of fishing them. When the fish are active and aggressive — but not spooky — and when the water temperature is right, using a greased line technique can certainly be a lot of fun. Over the years I've caught fish on the Kalama, the Salmon, and the Washougal rivers using this method.

Incidentally, I take notice that there are differences of opinion among steelhead and salmon anglers regarding the comparison between dry-fly and greased-line techniques. As far as I am concerned, any presentation in which the fly remains on the surface of the water is dry-fly fishing. If the fly sinks just under the surface of the water, then I consider that to be a wet-fly greased-line presentation.

The *riffling hitch*, also called the Portland Creek hitch, is a method of tying a wet fly onto the tippet so that it will skim or riffle across the surface of the water, creating a wake to attract fish in similar fashion to that produced by the waking technique with a dry fly. The fly is "hitched" by first tying the fly onto the tippet, then tying two additional half-hitch knots in the tippet material, and then tightening those additional knots down just behind the head of the fly.

I've never fished with a riffle hitch, simply because I've never encountered a situation in which I thought it would be particularly productive. However, it makes sense to me that a riffle hitch creating all that movement, wake, and motion ought to be a very good way to stimulate steelhead into a strike.

But keep in mind, we're all in the fly-fishing game for our own personal satisfaction. So despite what I might have to say about it, if using these techniques — or any other specialized dry-fly or wet-fly surface or near-surface techniques — are what you most enjoy in your fly fishing, then go for it! Take the time to read these books and learn these specialized fly and line manipulation techniques. There's a list in the back of some of my favorite steelhead fly-fishing books that include more detailed information on surface and just-under-the-surface fly presentations.

But that's not what this book is about. Because first and foremost for me, I like to catch fish, as many as I can. And I like to fish anytime — whatever the season of the year, the time of day, or the state of the weather. My fishing buddies and I are lucky to live near great steelhead and salmon rivers, and whenever we can, we will fish until darkness all day long throughout the year, in any kind of weather — high winds, freezing cold, rain, snow, even a blizzard — it doesn't matter. (Steelhead fishermen didn't develop their reputation for being crazy by staying home on the bad days!)

Out my way, fly fishermen take their steelhead and salmon fishing very seriously. That doesn't mean we're not going to practice good fly-fishing ethics right along. But there are not many purists among us. Make no mistake about it. When we're on the water, we're out there to catch fish, as many as we can, and the biggest we can. That means we're going to use the most effective fly-fishing tools and techniques we can. And for me and a lot of other very successful local anglers, we've learned that the name of the game is sub-surface wet flies.

It's a technique I also want to recommend to you, if you are among the majority of American anglers who live a relatively long distance away from steelhead and salmon water, and must plan your fishing trip months in advance without benefit of an accurate local weather forecast. Then months later, when you do make your trip, after having traveled a long distance to the Pacific Northwest (or the Great Lakes, for that matter), when you arrive you're going to have to fish in whatever weather and water conditions Mother Nature has dealt you at that time.

So my method of fishing for steelhead and salmon — what you are going to be reading about in this book — is designed for people like you and me: Fly fishermen who want to catch as many fish as they can on the fly rod, as well as those who, when they travel to steelhead and salmon fishing watersheds want to create the best possible odds they can to have a successful fishing trip, regardless of the weather, the condition of the water, or any other environmental aspect over which they have no control.

I believe that whatever fishing conditions you and I may encounter when we get streamside, day in, day out, *nothing is more reliable or more effective on steelhead and salmon — nothing will catch more fish! — than sub-surface presentations of wet flies.* Over the years, that's what I have been learning how to do reasonably well, I suppose, and that's the knowledge that I would like to share with you in the following pages.

I also believe in the expression, "Keep it simple, stupid!" I think many of our top fly fishers get so wrapped up in the great mystery and adventure of steelhead and salmon fishing that they tend to make the sport more complicated than it really is.

But it's really not. Think about this. To make an ethical catch on a steelhead or salmon (which means without deliberately snagging the fish) you've got to put your fly right in front of its mouth, or at least within a fairly small strike zone — say, two to four feet. Right? Because we have learned that unlike other fresh and saltwater species, steelhead and salmon will generally not move a long way to take a fly. So to get your fly in front of the fish's mouth, what has to happen?

First, you have to know that a fish is holding at the place where you're going to be presenting your fly. That is why, with these fish, you need to know a good deal about their life history, which is why I am going to devote a fair amount of space to that subject. Because unlike many other freshwater species, keep in mind that these are anadromous species that are *migrating.* Where the fish are going to be at any particular time depends upon a number of constantly changing variables: the status of their biological life cycle, the season of the year, the air and water temperatures, the water level, the chemistry of the river, and so on.

*Donna Teeny with a beautiful winter steelhead on the Three Rivers, located in Oregon.* ➤

Second, keep in mind that all steelhead and salmon rivers are not equal in quality; and that the quality of a particular watershed can change drastically over a period of time. Some of the most renowned steelhead and salmon rivers in memory are now, unfortunately, just that — a memory. So naturally, it is important that you take some time to study the history as well as the present day status of the steelhead rivers you want to fish. You should learn the location of the principal smaller tributaries on a river so you'll know just how far upstream the fish can go. Ask yourself the questions: What is the normal time for the peak spawning run? What are the bottom and bank conditions of this particular river? Some rivers have rock ledges and clay drop-offs, numerous slots and pockets in the current; others are more gravelly; some have large boulders which create faster-flowing pocket water; some rivers are relatively slow-moving, meandering. So knowing the topography and typical water flow characteristics of a river are important.

In the summer, for example, some rivers maintain a very low and placid water flow; whereas in the winter months they become large roaring streams. Each of these stream conditions requires differing fishing techniques. So having a good understanding of the rhythm of the seasons and the character and mood of the rivers is essential to success.

A thorough understanding of the life cycle of the migrating steelhead and salmon is also important. With steelhead, for example, timing is critical indeed. An angler simply cannot afford to be on the rivers either too early or too late. You have to learn how to keep the steelhead's schedule rather than your own. Good timing is based on knowing the lengths of the seasons and their effect on steelhead runs.

So assemble as much information as you can on the rivers you intend to fish well ahead of time. Talk to the appropriate state and federal fish and wildlife departments, collect and study hydraulic and climatic data, talk to local guides, and frequent the local fly-fishing shops, keeping in mind, always, that steelhead runs can differ dramatically from area to area.

Again — it's worth repeating — always research the rivers and streams you want to fish well in advance. Find out when the best runs of steelhead are in the river, when the runs peak, and what month you need to be on the river.

For example, Oregon's Salmon River, near Lincoln City, is known for its great winter run of steelhead. Its peak months are almost always December and January. After January, the fishing falls off drastically, so an angler fishing the Salmon in February hoping to get in on the winter steelhead is going to be disappointed.

On the other hand, the winter run on Oregon's Sandy River does not peak in December and January. On this watershed the winter run will continue to produce good fishing not only through February but often on into March and April.

\* \* \* \*

Despite what a lot of people will tell you, fly fishing for the anadromous salmon and trout — particularly steelhead — is simple. Note I didn't say "easy." It can be frustrating and hard, really hard, considering the quality of these great fish, the sometimes very difficult weather and watersheds where they thrive, and the techniques that must be mastered for consistent success. But, of course, therein lies the great fly-fishing challenge of these marvelous gamefish.

But I do try to follow a few basic rules, and I suggest you approach the sport in the same way.

First, when selecting my steelhead fishing sites, I like watersheds that have a lot of open spaces and several tributaries which will give me additional fishing opportunities. Make sure that the spot you pick also has available access points.

Second, once you're satisfied that there are fish in the stream you are fishing, you have to identify and locate one. That's why (as I will be discussing later in the book) I believe that sighted fishing is so critical to success on steelhead and salmon.

Third, once you've located your target fish, you have to place your fly sufficiently deep in the water column so that on its drift it will travel to a position just in front of the fish's mouth. And that means that whatever wet-fly pattern you are using — nymph, leech, or attractor — you must present it at the proper depth under the water. *Most steelhead and salmon, most of the time — particularly the big old males — do not hold close to the surface of the water unless they have to.* They much prefer to rest or hold in places where they don't have to fight against the current and are protected from predators, places such as deep pools, pockets, seam edges, riffles, and tail-outs from riffles.

Fourth, your fly needs to be a pattern that for whatever the reason (hunger, anger, curiosity . . . I don't care) the fish will decide to take a serious look at (and bite).

It's as simple as that.

As you read this book and others like it, and as you spend time on the stream gaining experience, you will, I hope, be introduced to and begin to master a number of specialized techniques that should improve your steelhead and salmon fishing. And there are many that can be learned. But don't be discouraged by that. No matter how complicated you want to make it, the sport will always remain, basically, the art of putting your fly in front of the fish.

So I'll repeat the premise of the book, the foundation of what my editors have chosen to call the Teeny technique: *nothing is more reliable and more effective on steelhead and salmon — nothing will catch more fish! — than sub-surface presentations of wet flies.*

Writing this book has been an interesting experience for me. It's not as much fun as fly fishing, but it did produce some special joys for me that I would like to acknowledge.

First, I would like to thank my friend, Doug Stewart, who provided the material for all the steelhead and salmon flies in the book (excepting my own Teeny patterns), and who personally tied the patterns that were used as models for the color photography.

Also, I would like to thank Amanda Adams, my editor at Odysseus Editions, for her patience, understanding, book publishing savvy, and absolute intolerance of anything even approaching second-rate. Every writer should be so lucky as to have an Amanda Adams looking over his shoulder.

Finally, for his invaluable support and counsel, I owe a huge debt of gratitude to my old friend — every fly fisherman's friend — the true master of them all, Lefty Kreh.

OVERLEAF: *A steelhead stream in northern California.*

## CHAPTER ONE

# A BRIEF NATURAL HISTORY OF STEELHEAD

Steelhead are simply polyanadromous rainbow trout, that is, they are migratory rainbow trout, whether they are sea trout or freshwater trout. They spawn in freshwater rivers and lakes, remain there for about two years, then migrate to the open sea where they will stay for another two to three years before they begin returning to their native rivers, thus completing the average steelhead life cycle.

As steelhead return to their home rivers, their years in the sea have brought them to full maturity and most of them will weigh between seven and 10 pounds. There are bigger steelhead than that, of course: fish that will have stayed in the ocean longer, feeding and growing, reaching impressive sizes of from 12 to 20 pounds or more.

Unlike the sea-run Pacific salmon, not all sea-run steelhead die immediately after spawning. Often as much as 15 to 20 percent of each steelhead generation that returns to freshwater to spawn for the first time will survive after spawning. These fish will recover from the harsh demands of the spawn and will eventually make their way back down the rivers and into the open sea again. But only a portion of these fish will survive their second migration to the ocean and return to their home rivers to spawn again. Not many will be strong enough to make these rare second spawning runs. And even that number is dwindling. Like all trout, steelhead face their share of problems, including continued loss of habitat, the increasing strains on their population from commercial fishing, the indiscriminate use of drift nets, polluted rivers, and the damaging effect of many dam constructions on their ancient migratory routes.

Steelhead running in the sea and lake steelhead look very much alike until the sea-run trout begin their migrations back into freshwater rivers and lakes to spawn.

There are few fish as physically beautiful as the sea-run steelhead. Those moving from the ocean back into the coastal rivers of the Pacific Northwest are a haunting silver in color, as bright as the flash of sunlight off summer rivers. You'll usually find that their side flanks are bright silver, their backs a darker gray. Many steelhead anglers call these trout "chrome bright," or "chromers." Indeed, they are so bright that they are often extremely difficult to see as they move into the rivers, where their bright silvery colors make them look almost translucent, like the color of the bright river water. You have to really concentrate and study the water when steelhead are in this color state; if you just casually glance over the surface, you'll miss them for sure.

After they have been in freshwater for a time, however, steelhead slowly begin to take on the color patterns of true rainbow trout, with various patterns of black spots sprinkled across their backs, complete with smears of red on the cheeks, with distinctive red stripes marking their flanks. These red stripes can range in color from soft coral pink to a deeper blood-red color. The males or bucks are more colorful than the females.

Another trait of the migratory rainbow, the steelhead, is that usually it will be somewhat smaller than the nonmigratory rainbow; trimmer, yet fierce and powerful.

Steelhead are an incredibly strong and wary fish, trout with an unyielding sense of survival. For a trout, they are exceptionally long lived, some surviving as long as seven years.

Along the Pacific Northwest coast, steelhead are constantly moving from the sea into the freshwater rivers. These migrations continue throughout the year, although the most active steelhead months are December, January, and March for winter steelhead; and June through August for the summer runs.

Steelhead are usually referred to by the predominate season when they move from the ocean into freshwater — spring, summer, fall, or winter. Although they vary in intensity, steelhead runs occur throughout the year. Most steelhead rivers have only a summer or a winter run; some have both. A number of the rivers of the Pacific Northwest experience no spring or summer steelhead runs at all. Some only host fall and winter-run trout. Others have both winter and spring/summer steelhead runs, and a few, mostly the big rivers, bustle with steelhead runs year-round. On Washington's Kalama River, for example, there is nearly a constant run of steelhead every month of the year.

Of course, steelhead don't make their spawning migrations on an exact calendar schedule, the way man plans his journeys. Boy, wouldn't we have better fishing if they did! From year to year, depending upon all sorts of variables, including weather, water level, water chemistry, etc., migrating dates will change, and there can even be an overlapping of seasons.

The spring-run steelhead, which generally enter freshwater commencing in early April, and the summer-run fish, which enter from June until August, enter freshwater as immature steelhead and remain there for up to a year before returning to the sea.

The winter steelhead are generally fully mature fish that enter freshwater rivers along the coast to spawn beginning in early December. Their spawning runs usually last through May. By far the greatest number of steelhead along the Pacific Northwest coast are winter steelhead, although the great runs above the Bonneville Dam on the Columbia River are made up of spring and summer fish.

After the spring fish enter the rivers, populations begin to mix and often by late May it is difficult to tell if you are taking spring steelhead or summer steelhead. The spring steelhead, like the fall fish (those that enter the river between September and November), should be smaller than the winter and summer fish. Depending upon their maturity, all of these fish will be spawning at the same time, from November through February, then again in March and April, and on and on, so the cycle is always wheeling, providing the Pacific Northwest with a thrilling year-round steelhead fishery.

But to make it simple, and really without sacrificing much in the way of comprehension, I like to think of the fish as simply having two seasonal runs: spring/summer-run steelhead (which includes both spring and summer-run fish) and winter-run steelhead (which would also include fall-run fish).

## WINTER STEELHEAD

In the Pacific Northwest, winter steelhead normally begin showing up at the mouths of their native rivers in mid-November. Usually, there are enough fish in the rivers by December to more than justify a day's fishing along many of the watersheds. The run becomes denser through January and February and into March. On some steelhead rivers, one of the best times for winter-run steelhead actually turns out to be March and early April.

As they enter freshwater, winter steelhead are ready to spawn, which is a major difference between winter steelhead and spring/summer-run fish. The winter fish are fully grown, sexually mature, well developed, carrying little, if any, excess body fat. They move up the rivers quickly, some spawning within a week of entering the river. In years with relatively normal water conditions, almost all of the winter-run steelhead have spawned within a month of returning to their home waters. These migrating winter fish are becoming very single-minded as they work their way into the rivers. All their energy is devoted to spawning.

It is generally believed that as these winter-run fish move upstream they stop feeding. For most fish, this is probably true, but I have seen many of these winter steelhead feed. For the most part, when they do feed, or strike a fly, they seem to do so out of habit and instinct rather than true hunger or driven desire. To me, their strike is often more impulse than anything else. It is this instinct — the steelhead's curiosity — that can work to the angler's advantage. Because even though every sense in their bodies is focused on sex, they will strike at a well-presented artificial fly.

But because they are so ready to spawn when they enter the rivers, the fish are also exceptionally wary, nervous, and incredibly difficult to catch. Indeed, of all the steelhead runs, winter steelhead seem to be, by far, the spookiest of the migratory steelhead of the Pacific Northwest. This is especially true when they are found in large numbers in shallow, clear water. Even the hint of a shadow moving across the water startles them, sending them scurrying.

If the winter-run steelhead are perhaps the greatest run of trout in terms of numbers, surely the spring/summer-run trout are the highest quality of all the migratory steelheads, quality both in looks — for they are a handsome fish — and in sporting quality on the rod.

Spring/summer steelhead will usually begin making their run for freshwater sometime in April or May. As they enter the rivers, the spring/summer-run steelhead are still sexually immature and they will spend more time in freshwater before they begin spawning, a spawn which mingles with many winter-run steelhead still in the rivers. Although most winter-run steelhead will spawn quickly and then return to the ocean, some do linger in the rivers throughout the winter and into the spring. The spring/summer-run trout are in no hurry and will often remain in the rivers through the summer months. Some steelhead will remain in freshwater for as long as eight or nine months.

When the spring/summer steelhead start their run for the rivers, they are even brighter and more difficult to see than winter steelhead. Spring/summer-run fish come in smaller numbers and are as difficult to see, in some instances, as bonefish are on the Florida flats. To find them, you have to know what to look for — an outline, a shadow, the sudden appearance of their white mouths, their distinctive flash as they roll in the river. Sometimes, as they roll, you often get a quick glimpse of the tail, as well.

These are heavy fish, their meat thick with stored fat, with a fierce edge to their mood and character. When spring/summer-run steelhead strike, they do so with a great deal more ferocity than winter-run trout. They can strip line faster than any other trout I know of. Even though they are in freshwater, they still fight like big saltwater fish, and once hooked they will often put on a bout of hydraulic acrobatics equal to that of the tarpon or Atlantic salmon.

My father used to tell me, "You haven't caught a steelhead until you've caught a springer!" And there's a lot of truth in those words. After I got my first one, I knew exactly what he meant because my legs were shaking and I could barely stand up after the battle was over. It was pretty awesome. They are indeed some kind of fish, bullet-shaped, beautiful and feisty, especially when they first enter the rivers. The spring/summer steelhead is one of the great gamefish of the world.

## THE PRINCIPAL STEELHEAD WATERS OF NORTH AMERICA

In the Pacific Northwest, almost all the remaining good steelhead rivers are north of San Francisco and the Russian River, including those in Oregon, Idaho, Washington, Vancouver Island, British Columbia, the southeastern coast of Alaska, as well as Alaska's lower Kenai Peninsula and several of its large coastal islands.

I was born in Portland, Oregon and these days my wife and I live in Gresham. It is true steelhead country, as is most of the Pacific Northwest coast north of California. As the list of rivers below clearly demonstrates, there are many great steelhead rivers throughout Oregon and Washington.

When I was a boy, my Dad and I did a lot of steelhead fishing along the waters of the Columbia River which forms much of the border between Oregon and Washington. Before dams were introduced on the Columbia, the steelhead would run upstream and into the Snake River and various tributaries, traveling even as far as Idaho, Wyoming, and Montana. The journey was difficult. But these were very strong and hearty fish. The Columbia was great steelhead water then; it still is.

In Oregon and Washington, the steelhead rivers can be exceptionally good, with runs of fish moving in the best of them throughout the year. Fish weighing 20 pounds, and even the occasional 30-pounder, while rare, are still possible; while steelhead running from six to 10 pounds are common. Considering the huge range of the anadromous Pacific steelhead, and the thousands of rivers, large and small, that are visited by the fish every year, it would take an encyclopedia to list them all. Just in Oregon, for example, the State Game Department classifies 162 winter-run steelhead rivers and 38 spring/summer-run steelhead rivers as suitable fly-fishing water. For purposes of this book, here is a partial listing of some of the most popular Pacific Northwest steelhead watersheds:*

OREGON

In Oregon, steelhead can be found on the Alsea, Chetco, **Clackamas**, **Columbia**, **Deschutes**, **Eagle Creek**, Grande Ronde, Hood, Illinois, Imnaha, John Day, **Kilchis**, Klamath, Lewis, McKenzie, **Miami**, Nehalem, **Nestucca**, North Umpqua, Rogue, **Salmon, Sandy**, Santiam, Siletz, Siuslaw, Sixes, Smith, Snake, South Fork of the Coquille, **Trask**, Umatilla, Umpqua, Walla Walla, Wallowa, **Willamette**, and **Wilson** rivers.

If I only had the time to sample one or two of Oregon's great steelhead watersheds, I suppose I'd choose the Deschutes or the Salmon rivers for spring/summer-run fish (the Salmon River near Lincoln City, Oregon is one of my favorite places); and the Sandy River for winter-run fish.

For the travelling fly fisherman whose business may bring him into the Pacific Northwest at anytime of the year, it is worth pointing out that we do have watersheds that can offer

---

*Jim's favorite steelhead rivers are shown in boldface. These rivers are also identified on the maps on pp. 33, 34, and 36 — *Editor.*

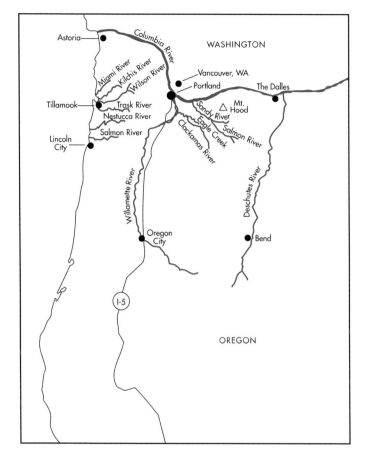

steelhead fly fishing year-round. The Clackamas, for example, has a winter/spring/summer/fall run of fish, as does the Sandy River (although in the summer when it is quite warm the Sandy is affected by glacial melt, becoming a milky color and very difficult to fish because of the low visibility). Other year-round steelhead rivers in Oregon include the Nestucca, the Wilson, and the Trask (although the number and vitality of Trask fish is lower in the spring and summer).

In Washington, the principal watersheds are the Chelalis, **Columbia, Cowlitz, Deschutes**, Dungeness, Elwha, Green, Hoh, Hoko, Humptulips, **Kalama, Klickitat, Lewis (North and East Forks)**, Nisqually, North Fork of the Stillaguamish, Pilchuck, Puyallup, Queets, Quinault, Samish, Sammamish, Sauk, Skagit, Skykomish, Snake, Snohomish, Snoqualmie, Sol Duc, Stillaguamish, Tolt, **Toutle, Washougal**, and **Wind** rivers.

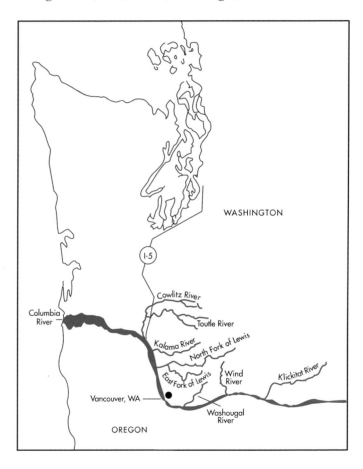

I caught my first steelhead on the Toutle River. (The character of the river was changed quite a bit by the Mt. St. Helens volcanic eruption, but I understand that the North Fork of the Toutle has come back very nicely and now has good runs in large numbers without heavy fishing pressure.)

Again for the travelling fly fisherman who may not be able to predict when he will be in the area, Washington offers several excellent year-round steelhead fisheries, including the Cowlitz, Kalama, Washougal, and the North Fork and East Fork of the Lewis River.

### CALIFORNIA AND IDAHO

Though I don't get a chance to get there as often as I would like, northern California has some fine steelhead watersheds. These include the Eel, Klamath, Mad, Mattole, Salmon, Scott, Shasta, Smith, Trinity, and Van Duzen rivers.

And in Idaho, there is still some good steelhead fishing on selected waters. I would certainly include the Clearwater, Salmon, and Snake rivers.

### BRITISH COLUMBIA

In British Columbia, there are literally hundreds of steelhead streams, probably some of which have never been fished. Some of the principal watersheds are the Alouette, **Babine**, Bella Coola, Blackwater, Brem, **Bulkley**, Capilano, Chehalis, Chilcotin, Chilko, Columbia, Copper, Coquihalla, Coquitlam, **Dean, Fraser, Kalum, Kispiox, Kitamat, Morice,** Nahatlach, Nicomekl, Powell, Seymour, Silver, **Skeena,** Squamish, **Sustut,** Telkwa, **Thompson, Vedder,** and Yakoun rivers.

For most steelhead anglers, the steelhead of British Columbia are perhaps the greatest steelhead in the world, exceptionally wary, wild, large, and beautiful. The great steelhead rivers of British Columbia — the wonderful Skeena River drainage, the Babine, the Bulkley, the Cooper, the incredible Kispiox

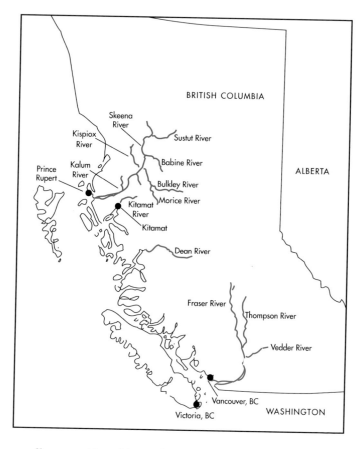

— all teem with wild, trophy-sized steelhead, trout that can reach 30, even 40 pounds.

For me, the best time to take on the steelhead of British Columbia is August, though the runs on the Dean, a coastal river, can be fished productively much earlier. Along the Skeena River system, though, July and August are the best months, especially mid-August, as the fish begin to move into the river and up the mouths of its tributaries in much the same fashion as steelhead move up the Columbia River. As the steelhead move upstream, the fishing action continually picks up, following the pulse of the spawn, with September and October being peak months, although the steelhead fishing in British Columbia can remain extremely active through November and into December.

Sometimes, the only thing that shuts the angling down on these waters is the cold, and with it the ice, which makes fishing difficult, if not impossible (not only because of surface ice, but also because of ice that forms in the rod guides). So, when it comes to steelhead fishing in British Columbia, the greatest uncertainty, the most perplexing variable, is the weather. It can make or break any trip. It can be beautiful and as perfect as any angler would want or absolutely miserable.

I've been steelhead fishing in British Columbia since the late 1950s and can honestly report that it is one of the most delightful and pleasurable of angling destinations. The countryside is not only beautiful, but still edged wildness. The people are kind, always helpful, and friendly. And, as I say, the steelhead fishing can be awesome.

The biggest steelhead I have ever taken on a fly in British Columbia came from the Kispiox, and weighed well over 25 pounds. I took a few big steelheads that day, all of them 19 pounds or bigger. Of the more than 20 steelhead John Dusa and I caught on the Kispiox that day, not one was under 16 pounds.

British Columbia's Vancouver Island also has a vigorous steelhead population in such watersheds as the Ash, Campbell, Capilano, Cowichan, Gold, Little Qualicum, Nanaimo, Nimpkish, Puntledge, Somass, Sproat, and Stamp rivers.

### ALASKA

Like British Columbia, Alaska has a huge number of steelhead watersheds — particularly along its southeastern coast — which have yet to be adequately explored and reported to the angling world. Some notable steelhead waters are the Karta

River near Prince of Wales, the watersheds near the town of Sitka, those north of Ketchikan, those on Kodiak Island, and those in the Yakutat area, notably the Situk River. There are also great little unnamed tributary creeks flowing into the Thorn Arm, a watershed about fifty miles south of Ketchikan.

## THE GREAT LAKES

In the Great Lakes, beyond the boundaries of their native Pacific coast fishery, stocking programs have considerably increased the range of steelhead over the years. Steelhead can be found today in all lands bordering upon the Great Lakes. Some of the streams flowing into the Great Lakes, most notably Michigan's Au Sable, Manistee, and Pere Marquette rivers, Minnesota's Bois Brule, and those streams on the north shore of Lake Superior in Ontario, have become superb steelhead (as well as salmon) habitats. In New York, the Salmon River, near Pulaski, is likely the most famous watershed for steelhead (as well as salmon and sea-run brown trout.) There are also a number of small rivers in the upper northeast corner of the state that do not experience a great deal of pressure and are worth exploring and fishing.

These Great Lakes steelhead have retained something of their native migratory cycle, and migrate from the deep, cold Great Lakes into their natal rivers and back again. And because their life cycle is so similar to that of the ocean-run steelhead of the Pacific coast, the Great Lakes steelhead are fished the same way. Since, basically, a steelhead is a steelhead, the same techniques and tackle apply, whether you're fishing for an ocean-run fish in Oregon or the landlocked (inland) variety in the upper midwestern and northeastern U.S.

## SMALL STREAMS

Although the big steelhead rivers get a lot of press, across the steelhead's entire range there are literally thousands of small streams that possess excellent steelhead runs. And it is not true that the biggest steelhead will necessarily be found in the biggest rivers, like the mighty Columbia. Indeed, often the largest fish — large being 20 or more pounds as I define it — will be found in the smaller rivers. Oftentimes, the water in these smaller watersheds (and their even smaller tributaries) is very low, making wading and sight fishing much easier and therefore more enjoyable; and there's generally less angling pressure. In Oregon, for example, such rivers would include the Chetko and Nehalem Rivers; in Washington, the Kalama, Quinault, Skagit, East Fork of the Lewis, and Washougal rivers. Fat with winter-run steelhead, the East Fork of the Lewis can produce fish of more than 25 pounds, while the Washougal is known for the quality of its spring/summer-run fish. Fish of 12 to 15 pounds are common during the river's spring/summer run. The lovely Kalama is also known for its quality steelhead and for yielding better than average-sized fish.

## STEELHEAD SIZE

The size of steelhead will vary from river to river. But of this I am certain: the world's biggest steelhead, great sag-bellied creatures, are to be found exclusively in the rivers of British Columbia and southeastern Alaska. It's as if this extremely wild country produces a strain of steelhead all its own. For example, a 42-pound fish, measuring 43 inches in length, was caught on hardware tackle at Bell Island, near Ketchikan, Alaska; and on the fly rod, most world records — ranging from 24 to 33 pounds — have been taken on the Sustut, Skeena, and Kispiox rivers of British Columbia.

Meanwhile, farther to the south, in the steelhead fisheries of Oregon, Washington, Idaho, and California, the steelhead for the most part tend to be trimmer and leaner. This is not to say that these southern steelhead never chunk-up, though. I have caught many a winter-run Oregon steelhead that was blunt or bullet-shaped, with a dragging belly.

Generally speaking, when it comes to steelhead size, trophy fish usually start at about 12 pounds. Incidentally, if you're caught on the water without a tape measure or scale, a good rule of thumb for measuring the weight of a steelhead is that, usually, a 24-inch steelhead will normally weigh about 5 pounds; a 30-inch fish will normally weigh about 10 pounds. For steelhead measuring greater than 30 inches, you should add a pound for each additional inch, up to, say, 36 inches. After steelhead reach 36 inches in length, they tend to be heavier than they look, because at that size their girth is becoming disproportionate to their length. So, using this rule of thumb, a 36-inch steelhead should weigh 15 pounds. But when the girth of this very large steelhead is taken into account, it may very well weigh from 18 to 20 pounds. Also, this pound-per-inch formula is of no use at all with the very large British Columbia and southeastern Alaska steelhead, which as I've discussed above, are stouter than other steelhead populations and really in a class by themselves. For example, a big British Columbia steelhead with a length of 38 inches and a girth of 20 inches will almost certainly weigh at least 21 pounds. With these fish, as the girth measurement goes up, there is a dramatic gain in weight. A British Columbia steelhead with a girth of 23-inches would be a big steelhead indeed.

## STEELHEAD HABITAT

### WATER TEMPERATURE

Just as steelhead exist satisfactorily in a wide array of water conditions, so can they do very well in a wide range of water temperatures. (And incidentally, for the balance of this discussion of steelhead habitat, I am referring to the northwestern Pacific range of the fish, as this is the country with which I am familiar.) Like brown trout, steelhead will remain active and productive in water temperatures up to 70 degrees Fahrenheit. Even so, they like colder water. Prime water temperatures for steelhead, I've found, seem to be from the mid-40s to the low 60s. In this temperature range you will find the healthiest fish, the most active fish, the biggest fish.

And just as they can stand extremes of warm water, so can steelhead survive in extremes of cold water. I have taken steelhead from water barely above freezing. But this extremely cold water (as well as extremely hot water) makes them exceptionally lethargic, holding in deeper water, barely moving at all, and difficult to catch. Almost nothing interests them. Indeed, any fly cast to them will have to be presented almost perfectly. And that means, in such extremely cold or extremely hot water temperatures, that you need to make sure your fly is drifting very slowly in the water column. Because the fish are so lethargic, they will simply not be too interested in chasing a fast-moving fly. And if you do get lucky enough to catch one, don't expect a spectacular battle.

### AIR TEMPERATURE

Steelhead fishing can be wild. That's the reason most steelhead fishermen exhibit such crazy behavior. Particularly in the winter. Following the great beauty of fall in the Pacific Northwest, the winter comes quickly and its grip on the countryside and rivers is firm and abiding. Normal winters in the Pacific Northwest will bring temperatures in the 40s, with some days actually warming into the 50s and 60s. Likewise, there can be days or weeks of freezing, miserably cold weather, with temperatures dropping into the 30s, even into the 20s.

Winter usually means lower, clearer water on the rivers and, of course, colder water. But even if the weather is not the most pleasant and comfortable, the steelhead fishing is often at its best, and a good steelhead run is certainly worth a little discomfort. Don't you agree?

Springtime in the Pacific Northwest is genuinely beautiful. As the temperatures warm, the spring thaw or run-off begins and river levels begin to rise, slowly but steadily, until early summer. With the rising water comes warming air and water temperatures, the daily averages settling somewhere in the mid-60s up into the 70s.

The summer season provides optimum weather with average temperatures in the Oregon/Washington area in the 70s and 80s. I like the summer season because the rivers are more stable — with low and clear water. These nice water conditions continue into the fall season, which is even more beautiful with the fall's foliage change.

## Water Clarity

A fly fisherman has his best possible chance with moving steelhead when the watershed he is fishing is clean and relatively clear. The clearer the better. Clear water enables you to make out ledges and pocket water, and there is usually the chance of actually seeing the fish and watching them move throughout the watershed. Unfortunately, not all steelhead rivers are clean and clear. Weather can turn them turgid and muddy. Pollution can discolor them, even ruin them.

Any tint to the water can make the fishing more difficult. But, sometimes, darker water can work to the angler's advantage. In dark water you can use shorter and heavier leaders and bigger flies, all without fear of spooking the fish. Darker water also means you don't have to be so self-conscious about what color clothing you wear on the river. (On clear, bright steelhead water, you really have to pay attention to the color of your clothing. On such clear water, a wrong-colored shirt will spook a fish as easily as a bad cast.)

Come fall, dark water becomes a detriment. The steelhead rivers become darker then because of the seasonal changes in nature, taking on the taint and colors of the multitude of falling leaves. Many of the Pacific Northwest rivers become tea-colored at this time. When the leaves first begin to fall — especially if rain is added to the situation — fly fishing can be really difficult, a real challenge. Even the very best angler is going to spend much of his time catching and releasing mats of leaves. It's best to wait out the peak of the leaf fall, until the rivers begin to clear again. As they do, their waters will be darker, the color of dull bronze, but fishable.

Dams can have a poor effect upon steelhead populations. This is especially true of the smaller fish. In Idaho, fishery experts are working around this by letting young steelhead go well below the great Bonneville Dam, the lowest dam on the Columbia River. The fish seem to do a lot better this way, returning in greater numbers to the ocean and then returning to the river in much better shape, healthier, and bigger. Maintaining the fish in heavily oxygenated water seems to make a big difference in the success of their life cycle. For steelhead, as with all trout, moving water, water rich in oxygen, is absolutely vital.

Steelhead can survive, even thrive, both in natural, unobstructed rivers as well as dammed rivers. Where dams exist, however, for the fish to survive, they absolutely must have fish ladders so that they can get upstream and down easily. Ladders were absent from most older dams, but these days, on rivers heavily used by migratory fish, few if any dams are approved for construction that do not include fish ladders or diversionary dams, like the one on Oregon's Sandy River, which gives the steelhead and water a way of by-passing the dam and running directly into Roslyn Lake.

Naturally, the best steelhead river is the river that is left in its natural state — free-flowing. These watersheds provide the fly fisherman with the unmatched experience of being able to fish for steelhead in nearly wild and pristine conditions. There are still some free-flowing rivers in the Pacific Northwest. Just to name a few:

In Oregon, I would certainly include the Kilchis, Miami, Nestucca, Sandy, Santiam, Salmon, Trask, and Wilson rivers. The Sandy River does have one diversion dam, but it is accompanied by a fish ladder so it could really be classified as a free-flowing river.

In Washington, the Kalama and the Washougal are what I consider to be free-flowing rivers. I would also include the East Fork of the Lewis, though it has incredibly beautiful natural falls that provide a very difficult obstacle for the fish to navigate. Yet, surprisingly, when they finally elect to travel up the falls, the fish perform best during low water because there is less volume and flow of water coming down the falls at that particular time.

The Wind River also has natural water falls which are almost impossible to pass and very few fish are able to accomplish the feat. Here, the fish management people have constructed a small fish ladder. Aside from that, I regard the Wind as basically a free-flowing river.

In British Columbia, the Bulkley, Copper, Dean, Kispiox, Morice, Skeena, Sustut, and Vedder rivers are all without obstruction. There are some diversion dams on these river systems, but no hydro-electric constructions. Thus, I consider these rivers to be free-flowing because they're not being mechanically controlled.

Also, since the coastal area waters of most rivers in Oregon, Washington, and British Columbia have no dams, they should also be regarded as free-flowing.

Other important variables that are going to influence your fly-fishing success are the amount of pollution, the amount of oxygen, the speed of the current flow, and the level of the water. When it comes to steelhead, I certainly prefer low water. It is easier to wade and therefore considerably safer, even though the steelhead are much spookier. Also, low water is easier to read and easier to study and fish.

OVERLEAF: *Jim Teeny poses with a fall-run chinook on the Trask River in Oregon.*

CHAPTER TWO

# A BRIEF
# NATURAL HISTORY
# OF THE
# PACIFIC SALMON

Few species of fish equal the Pacific salmon for their impact on mankind. There are five major species: the chinook, coho, sockeye, pink, and chum (plus two relatively rare species found only in Japan and parts of the USSR, the *masa*, or cherry salmon, and the *biwa* salmon). Because they must return to their freshwater natal rivers to spawn, millions of these fish migrate annually to the west coast of North America and the east coasts of Japan and the USSR.

Prior to the coming of the white man, the North American Indian enjoyed a rare advantage for the wilderness hunter, his food supply came to him every year. Indian tribes relied upon these fish as their principal food source, and established permanent settlements on the best salmon waters where they could easily net and smoke enough salmon to meet the entire annual food requirement of their populations.

After the exploration and colonization of the Pacific Northwest by the white man, as early as the mid-nineteenth century the Pacific salmon similarly became a major food source and thriving commercial industry of the civilized world. Early commercial fishermen used a variety of capture techniques, including the construction of weirs and large floating traps, as well as gill-nets, long lines, purse seines, and trolling.

Side by side with the commercial fishermen came the sport angler, who recognized immediately that all of these relatively large fish — ranging from the very large chinook with an average weight of about 20 to 30 pounds, to the small pink salmon, with an average weight of about four pounds — could provide superb sport. Either by long-line fishing or trolling with baitfish, plugs, or spoons in the saltwater; or by fly fishing at the mouths of estuaries and the upstream reaches of hundreds of natal freshwater rivers and tributaries.

Traditionally, the major sport fish of fly fishermen has been the coho (silver) salmon. However, more and more anglers are coming to realize that, if fished in the proper way with the right-sized tackle, chinook, chum, pink, and sockeye can also offer superb fly-fishing action.

All the Pacific salmon are anadromous, and share a common life cycle of being born and then dying after only one spawn in their freshwater natal river or tributary. They are hatched from eggs that have been deposited in a shallow gravel nest (or redd) by the female and fertilized by the male. As the parent fish begin their dying process, the new generation of salmon hatch and enter the world in a form known as alevin, with the yolk of their egg sack still attached to their bodies. In various time frames that can vary widely from species to species and from year to year, the balance of the salmon's life cycle will be completed: the yolk is absorbed and the alevin becomes a free-swimming fry; the fry grows into a smolt; the smolt journeys to the ocean where as a mature fish it will spend the major portion of its life; it then returns back to its freshwater birthplace where it spawns and dies.

In their anadromous migration from freshwater to saltwater and back to freshwater again, the Pacific salmon have been known to travel vast distances across the ocean, sometimes as much as 2,500 miles. And the freshwater spawning journey of some species can be equally impressive. For example, while it is common for salmon spawning grounds to be found fairly close to that point in the river where tidal effect ends, some redds are located hundreds of miles from the ocean. Chinook salmon, for example, are known to travel as much as 1,200 miles upstream to spawning grounds in the headwaters of the Yukon River.

Along with the migrations of certain birds, one of life's great unsolved mysteries is, of course, the ability of an individual salmon to travel hundreds or even thousands of miles from deep in the ocean ultimately to home in on its shallow freshwater place of birth and death. Considerable research has been done, and many theories involving current flow, sea-water temperature, salinity, and other biological factors have been advanced, to explain the salmon's extraordinary navigation system. Salmon are now known to have iron-rich areas of the brain, which are believed to aid in magnetic navigation. There is also the recent theory that a salmon's natal water gives off a distinctive odor that the fish can detect. But surely it cannot detect the odor of a freshwater stream 1,000 miles offshore in the deep ocean! Or can it? On this fascinating mystery, man has some clues, but no solution.

Salmon life cycles are often quite similar to that of the steelhead. And just as with migrating steelhead, to increase your chances for success, you have to really study and get to know the salmon rivers you are going to fish before you fish them. You need to know the river's cycles, whether it hosts only one seasonal spawning run or several runs.

Pacific salmon runs are somewhat different once you leave the Lower 48 and travel north to the waters of British Columbia and Alaska. For example, the best month to fish for salmon in Alaska is June through July, when on some days, you can fish for chinook, chum, and sockeye at the same time. And during the even years, pink salmon will be there, as well, making their biennial run. For this reason, many salmon fishermen of the Pacific Northwest will fish Alaska in the summer and then, come the fall, fish Oregon and Washington for the same species.

Timing is critical with Pacific salmon. If you hit them at the right time, then you will be fishing incredible numbers of fish. If you're a week off, though, either early or at the tail end of the run, you will see fewer fish.

CHINOOK SALMON

The great chinook salmon of the Pacific Northwest is also known as King salmon, *Oncorhynchus tshawytscha*. It is the largest of the Pacific salmon. It varies greatly in size. On rare occasions, anglers have hooked tremendous chinooks, fish weighing well over 100 pounds. On average, however, chinook salmon will run from 15 to perhaps 50 pounds.

The heavily muscled back of mature chinook salmon is marked by fields of black spots, spots of random sizes, and an array of irregular shapes. Dark spots also mark the chinook's dorsal fin and the lobes of the caudal fin. Another distinctive trait of mature chinooks is the blackened gums at the base of their teeth.

As is true with most species of Pacific salmon, there are several varieties of chinook salmon, each distinguished by the time of the year the fish make their spawning run from the sea back into the freshwater rivers along the coast. Some chinook salmon make an early run, entering their home rivers sometime in January. Others will not make their run until well into the fall. In any event, chinook salmon are usually on the move throughout the year and, like migratory steelhead, are known simply as spring, summer, fall, and winter salmon, with the summer and fall runs being crossovers; that is, summer runs will include spring fish and fall runs will include winter fish.

Most anglers consider the chinook to be a spring salmon. When the spring chinook enter the rivers, they are already big fish, weighing from 12 to 25 pounds, on average, with some smaller and some as large as 30 pounds or more. And all of these early chinook are high quality fish — fat, heavy, and ready to spawn.

Chinook salmon generally spawn in larger rivers or larger tributaries, near riffles. They tend to spawn in deeper water and on larger gravel than the other Pacific salmon. But there doesn't seem to be a consistent pattern to their choice of a spawning site. For example, along the Columbia River, spring chinooks prefer spawning at the mouths of tributaries of smaller rivers rather than the main channel, while the fall chinooks are just the opposite, preferring the main channel of the big river to the calmer waters of its tributaries.

Incidentally, the many dams that have been constructed along the Columbia and its watershed have created a great many problems for the spawning salmon. Indeed, while the steelhead fishing remains good on the Columbia, most of the quality salmon spawning water along its watershed has been ruined, altered, or completely eliminated.

Up along the salmon waters of Canada, where these fish can grow to 40 pounds or more, chinooks are often called tyee (or spring) salmon. The tyees are the big chinooks. Smaller chinooks, called jack salmon, usually weigh from two to eight pounds. The chinooks that range in size somewhere between the smaller jacks and the monster tyees, or say, about 12 pounds or more, are generally referred to as King salmon. Fish weighing from 25 to 45 pounds are routinely caught on the fly. A fish over 50 pounds would be rare, while there have been reports of Alaska chinooks weighing as much as 120 pounds, and of a record fish of 97 pounds landed on hardware tackle on Alaska's Kenai River in 1985. On the fly rod, many of the largest chinooks have been harvested on Oregon's Chetco River, while the fly rod record is a 63-pound King caught on Oregon's Trask River.

During their spawning runs, chinook salmon hold their weight much better than most other spawning salmon. This is especially true of the females, who still look shiny and fat as they move up their native rivers. Well into the spawning season, the males will begin to go almost completely black, take on a slightly haggard look, while the females become the color of polished bronze.

The color scheme of the chinook is considered unique among Pacific salmon because there are two distinct phases. While most exhibit the bold red color associated with spawning salmon, as much as 20 to 30 percent of the chinook population sport a silver-white coloring.

Like most everything else in nature, maturity is a variable among chinooks. Growth from alevin to fry to smolt can be a quick process or a slow one. Some males will reach full-blown maturity in a year; for others, full maturity may take as long

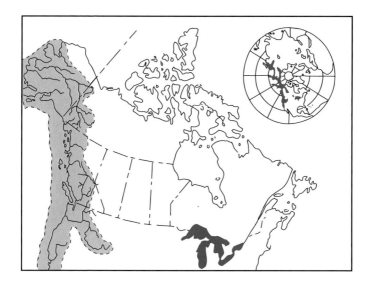

*The Range of Chinook Salmon*

as six to eight years. Likewise, chinook tend to move to the sea in random spurts rather than following a set cycle. Some chinook leave for the sea as soon as they are able. Some remain in their home rivers for months before making their way to the sea. Generally, however, among chinooks, fall fish head for the sea before they reach five months of age. Spring salmon tend to remain in freshwater for longer periods of time. Some spring chinooks will not leave for the sea until they are more than a year old. After four to six years at sea, the salmon return to their native rivers.

The chinooks are great salmon and have a wide range. They can be found as far east as the Great Lakes of the United States; as far west as the Bering Strait, the Okhotsk seas, and the Sea of Japan; as far south as the Ventura River in California; and as far north as Point Hope, Alaska, and the Arctic Ocean. But the bigger chinooks, the big Kings, are mostly found in the waters of the Pacific Northwest as well as Idaho, Alaska and British Columbia.

Attempts have been made to establish chinook populations in many areas around the world, but most have been unsuccessful. Aside from their native Pacific Northwest, Alaska, and the north Pacific rim of Russia, chinooks have only been able to survive as a self-supporting anadromous population in the Great Lakes (where they initially thrived but are now failing to maintain spawning populations), in Chile (which I understand is beginning to maintain a very successful fishery), and on the South Island of New Zealand.

Sea-run chinooks can travel great distances. Studies of tagged fish show that some of these salmon will journey more than 2,000 miles to return to their home waters. This is especially true of Alaska chinooks, which are generally found in the big river systems and tend to spawn from summer through November.

In the Pacific Northwest, the chinook salmon remains the dominant salmon for the sports fisherman, both in terms of numbers of fish and pounds of fish. Its popularity far outweighs that of the other Pacific salmon. Also, the salmon rivers of Oregon and Washington and northern California still account for a healthy percentage of the chinook salmon taken each year by sport fishermen.

But the great growth of chinook populations has not occurred naturally. The chinook has received a lot of help from man. It has proved to be a fish that reproduces easily and quickly in hatcheries, and since the late 1970s millions of hatchery chinook have been released throughout the salmon waters of the Pacific Northwest, so that despite the presence of man-made dams and thousands of sport and commercial fishermen, there are now more chinook salmon in the waters of the Pacific Northwest than ever before — most of them hatchery-created fish.

COHO SALMON

*Oncorhynchus kisutch*. A mouthful and a handful: as are all true salmon. Like all salmon of the Pacific Northwest, the coho goes by several names, including silver and hooknose salmon. Sea-run coho are among the most powerful of salmon and are known for their ferocity and their tenacity. It is one of the most sought after gamefish species for the fly fisherman.

Coho are bright, silvery fish when they enter freshwater, and at this time will take a fly readily. But as they move upstream to spawn, changing into their spawning colors very rapidly, with each day closer to spawning time it becomes more and more difficult to persuade the coho to take a fly. Initially, however, when they first come into the rivers they are a fierce fish and a great fly-fishing challenge. If a coho salmon can be hooked fresh from the ocean just as it leaves saltwater, when it is fresh, strong and quick to respond, it can provide an aggressive, leaping fight that many anglers believe to be the equal of the Atlantic salmon.

The color of pounded silver, cohos also flash a wide array of dark spots, especially on their backs, their tail, and along the edges of the caudal fin. The teeth, plentiful and sharp, are embedded in thick white gums.

There is normally only one seasonal run of coho, the big summer-to-fall run that on some watersheds will extend into November and December. In the Pacific Northwest, the coho will start appearing in huge schools off the coastal rivers in late summer, sometime in July and August, and anglers will be waiting at the river mouths to catch them. However, in some areas on the West Coast, spawning runs can start as early as May or as late as December. In the Great Lakes, coho spawning runs occur from late September into early October.

Though there appears to be no hard rule, most young cohos generally do not move into the sea until they are a full year old. Some will move sooner; others may stay in their natal river as long as two years. During their river lives, coho delight in sticking to deep pools, hanging away from the river's current. Here they stay, content, until they suddenly turn silver and head for the sea. In the saltwater, they grow at a tremendous rate for perhaps two to three years, reach their full maturity, and just as suddenly begin their migration back to freshwater. Up to 90 percent of cohos manage to make it back to their natal rivers for the spawn.

Although coho salmon, as a species, have a wide range, being found in waters from northern California to the sea off Japan, individual populations stay close to their native rivers. While there have been captures of tagged fish as far as 1,200 miles from their tagging site, coho do not migrate the vast distances of chinook, generally not more than 150 miles or so from their natal water.

On their spawning runs, coho generally penetrate upriver beyond the spawning beds of sockeye, pink, and chum salmon, sometimes utilizing the entire length of smaller rivers. They prefer the shallow, gravelly areas of swift water for their spawning nests. Not all cohos are anadromous, and in some lakes and streams can be found fish that have never migrated to the sea.

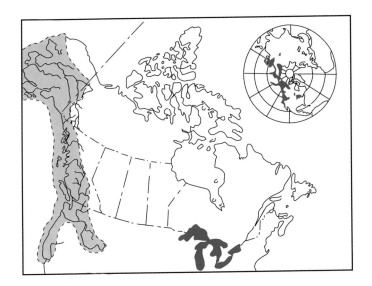

*The Range of Coho Salmon*

Coho salmon have an excellent survival record. Many experts believe that is because so many of them spawn in small coastal rivers, where there is less pressure on them. Also, their migrations are much shorter and much less hazardous than that of the chinook, for example.

Coho salmon occur naturally only in the Pacific Ocean and its tributary drainages. Like chinook salmon, the fish are widely distributed. In North America, they range from the waters of Monterey Bay in California, through California, Oregon, Idaho, Washington, British Columbia, and Alaska.

On the continent of Asia, coho salmon can be found from the Anadyr River in the USSR, south to Hokkaido, Japan. Since 1967, when coho smolts were introduced into watersheds in Michigan, New York, and Ontario, Canada, the Great Lakes area has become an immense popular and successful coho salmon fishery.

Coho salmon are smaller than chinooks. The largest coho ever caught on rod and line, weighing over 33 pounds, was recorded in 1970 on the Little Ministee River, Michigan, but the average fish weighs from eight to 12 pounds. Cohos over 12 pounds are uncommon, and fish in the 15-pound range should be considered real trophies.

After the rainbow trout, in Alaska — where it is called the silver salmon — the coho is probably the most popular fly-rod fish, and the catch of 50 fish in a day on a fly rod is an achievable goal.

In the Pacific Northwest, the coho is second only to the chinook in salmon population. Great numbers of fish — often more than 300,000 — used to be taken each year from the salmon rivers of Washington, Oregon, and northern California. In recent years, coho runs are way down in this region, but various protection plans are being formulated to increase coho numbers in the Pacific Northwest watersheds.

SOCKEYE SALMON

The sockeye salmon, *Oncorhynchus nerka*, is a great sporting fish, as well as my favorite type of salmon for the dinner platter. A lot of people must agree, because it is the salmon that

*The Range of Sockeye Salmon*

keeps the canneries running full tilt during the commercial fishing season

Spawning sockeye put on some show, gathering in their home rivers in great hordes. When they arrive, these rivers will boil with their frenzied activity. There have been years when places like Bristol Bay, Alaska, have teemed with millions upon millions of sockeye.

Also known as the red salmon, sockeye are a favorite gamefish for me. Its range is similar to that of the other Pacific salmon, but more abbreviated. In North America, its natural fishery extends from the Klamath River in California up the Pacific Northwest coast to Alaska and as far as Bathurst Inlet in the Arctic Ocean. It is also found in Asia from northern Hokkaido, Japan, to the Anadyr River in the USSR.

Many American fly fishermen will also be familiar with a dwarf landlocked species of sockeye, which is the kokanee salmon. The kokanee salmon is almost identical to the sockeye salmon in its biological make-up and appearance, except that it is somewhat smaller, is not anadromous, and spends none of its life in the ocean.

The natural range of the kokanee covers essentially the same territory as the sockeye — particularly in British Columbia and the Yukon Territory — although kokanee will also occur naturally in many lakes to which the anadromous sockeyes have no access. Also, kokanee salmon have been successfully introduced into a number of lakes and streams across the northern tier of the United States and in Canada.

Maturing anadromous sockeye salmon returning to spawn appear in the coastal waters of the Pacific Northwest from May to October. Among their favorite spawning locales are gravel beds along the shore of the inlets of lakes. Unlike other species of Pacific salmon, most sockeye populations require a river system that includes sizable lakes, where the sockeye will smolt before going to sea for up to three years. But this is not a fixed rule of behavior. Some sockeyes will spawn in big rivers without lakes.

As gamefish, it's best to take on sockeye before they have traveled too far upriver on the spawn, before they have taken on their full mating colors — an unmistakable blister red and nearly black-green.

Rather, if you can, take them when they are bright and vibrant, full of power and energy, flashing silver in the cold river. Indeed, at first they look a great deal like ocean-run steelhead, though they are a much stronger fish, pound-for-pound. You can immediately tell the difference between a 10-pound sockeye and a 10-pound steelhead: the sockeye simply has more power, more endurance and more strength. They are truly awesome fighters. But they are not easy fish to catch on a fly

*A Pacific salmon river in Alaska.* ➤

rod. I recognize my opinion is contrary to what you may have heard from fly fishermen returning from Alaska and reporting that there was no sport in fly fishing for sockeye. All they had to do was cast their fly into a big school of spawning sockeyes, and they got a hook-up every time. They might have gotten a hook-up on every cast, but I'll bet most of those "hook-ups" were snags!

However for me, fished in an ethical manner, there is no Pacific salmon more challenging than the sockeye. I guarantee that if you are able to get a well-drifted fly at the right depth in front of a sighted sockeye, and if that fish takes your fly in its mouth, you are going to be in for one of the world's greatest fly-fishing treats!

For great sockeye runs, Alaska is the place and July is the month. Often the sockeye will appear there in enormous pods along the coast and then enter the rivers where there will be so many of them that the surface of the water will seem to bubble and boil with fish — hundreds of them rolling on the surface at once! Once hooked, a fresh sockeye really takes off, ripping out line and putting on a grand show. It is something every angler should see at least once: its crazed runs, its marvelous leaps out of the water. Which, given its smaller size, is all the more amazing.

While somewhat larger than pink salmon, sockeye are not big fish. On average, migrating sockeye will weigh from four to perhaps nine pounds. The record sockeye, caught in Alaska, weighed close to 16 pounds. And believe me, a 16-pound sockeye is equal to a 30 or 40-pound chinook in terms of its fight and fierce determination. Any sockeye over 10 pounds should be considered a trophy.

I love them! I love to fly fish for them! I believe sockeye salmon are the most underrated fish in the fly-fishing world. I caught my first one in Alaska in 1975 and have been hooked on them ever since.

CHUM SALMON

If the sockeye is all beauty and grace, the chum or dog salmon is surely the ugliest salmon of them all — particularly after it has been on the spawn for sometime. With its strange yellow-green calico markings and its rows of threatening teeth, you'll never mistake a chum for any other critter in the world.

Chum salmon, *Oncorhynchus keta*, are noted for being Pacific salmon without a distinctive array of black spots. Instead, chum salmon are marked by fins edged in black (all except the dorsal fin, which is free of any such markings) and a beautiful splash of dark streaks on their backs and bellies. Before spawning, chum salmon are a pale iridescent green.

Like sockeye, chum salmon are bright fish as they enter their native rivers. Their markings are, at this time, still dim, only beginning to deepen, only beginning to take on their distinctive definition and color. As they continue their spawning run, chum, which begin as very powerful fish, with a vigorous strike, begin to break down and weaken. In appearance, they become anything but handsome; they take on a completely tattered and haggard look.

Compared to other Pacific salmon, chums are more sexually mature when they arrive at the mouth of their spawning streams, and therefore they frequently spawn in tidal water. Apparently they do not possess the ability of the other Pacific salmon to overcome river obstructions, and therefore generally do not penetrate rivers more than 100 miles or so. It is generally believed that most chum salmon — especially the summer fish — spawn in the lower reaches of their home waters. But in several rivers, such as Alaska's Yukon, chums have been sighted as far upriver as the headwaters, which means that some of these salmon are capable of long migrations covering more than 2,000 miles. And we do know that chums also move far up the Babine, Kuskokwim, and Mackenzie rivers.

Even so, the lives and the comings and goings of chum salmon are still filled with a great deal of mystery. Their populations can and often do fluctuate dramatically. In some years, great numbers of chum salmon will move in from the sea; other years there may be just a few sightings of newly spawning fish in tidal waters. Scientists believe that basically there are summer and fall chum salmon, and that the full cycle of a generation of chum salmon covers from four to five years.

The summer chum salmon is generally smaller than the fall fish and tends to spawn and mature earlier. Also, its migrations seem to be somewhat shorter, covering less territory. Summer chum salmon begin entering their home rivers in the Pacific Northwest in the summer, around July, and the spawning run will continue through December. In northern British Columbia, the fish will arrive at the river estuaries as early as July. In southern British Columbia, the chum spawn is somewhat later, beginning in September and continuing until January.

The fall run of chums generally consists of larger fish, and in greater numbers, than the summer run. These fall-run chum salmon can be impressive indeed, some going well into the 20-pound range.

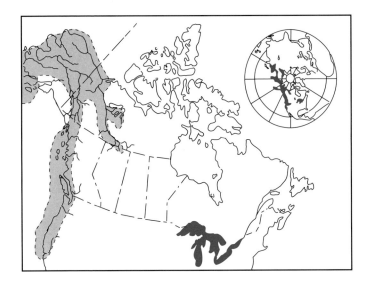

*The Range of Chum Salmon*

The environment of their natal river apparently greatly influences the size, life cycle, and behavior of chum salmon. A comparison between two specimens taken from different rivers may reveal quite dissimilar characteristics. Bigger chum salmon, for example, are caught more often in the rivers of Oregon, Washington, and British Columbia, than in Alaska.

In some watersheds, chums make their spawning run at about the same time as chinook and sockeyes, so that on these rivers it is possible to fish for all three of these species of Pacific salmon at the same time.

As a general rule, in most Pacific Northwest watersheds, the average weight of a mature chum salmon will be from about eight to 11 pounds. A 33-pound fish has been reported from Canada, and the fly-rod world record is just under 24 pounds. Chum weighing in excess of 12 pounds should be considered trophy fish.

Like the coho salmon, the species ranges widely. The chum's natural range around the Pacific basin extends, in North America, from the Sacramento River in California along the Oregon, Washington, British Columbia, and Alaska coasts to the Bering Strait; as well as the Asian waters of the Okhotsk Sea, the Sea of Japan, all the way to Korea. In the Arctic Ocean, its range extends west to the Lena River, and east to the Peel and Mackenzie Rivers.

Few attempts have been made to transplant chums to other waters of the world. In 1955, unsuccessful attempts were made to introduce the species to the watersheds of the Hudson Bay and James Bay, in Canada.

Regarding its name, some say the chum salmon has been given its alternative name, dog salmon, because of its awesome dentistry. Others say it's because the Eskimos will feed their dogs chum salmon to get them through the winter when meat is scarce.

Among most American fly fishermen, the chum salmon is not highly prized as a gamefish, primarily, I believe, because many chum reach our freshwater rivers for spawning late in the fall, when temperatures have fallen considerably and a number of fly fishermen have ceased fishing for the season. In addition, their spawning runs leave chum salmon with the most haggard and unappealing appearance of all the Pacific salmon. As I've said before, no chum will ever win a salmon beauty contest.

But whatever their appearance late in their spawning cycle, if you can hook a chum bright and fresh from the ocean, it can be a truly violent, unyielding fish, the kind that breaks not only a lot of leaders, but a lot of rods. It's not uncommon to see a few stray lines floating on Oregon's Kilchis River, out of Tillamook Bay, from a fly fisherman's failed encounter with a chum. They are that strong. They are good biters and good fighters.

PINK SALMON

*Oncorhynchus gorbuscha* — pink salmon — take their name from the lovely and stunning color of their flesh, which is far less oily than that of the sockeye. That probably accounts for their taste, which in the opinion of most people is inferior to that of the other Pacific salmon.

Pinks spawn only every other year. Some strains or races of fish will spawn in even-numbered years; the others in odd-numbered years. Strains or races of fish which spawn in even and odd-numbered years can even occupy the same watershed; but in most rivers one strain will predominate. Also, if a strain has a dominant run in one year, in the next year its numbers will be substantially reduced. There may also be a significant difference in the date of return, as well as the age and weight, of individual fish of two different strains in different spawning rivers.

Curiously, those pink salmon born during odd-numbered years tend to populate the species' northern range, while those with an even-numbered year of birth tend to gather to the south. Also, quite unusually, while most pink salmon return to their home waters, some are wanderers and will spawn in an entirely different watershed from the one in which they

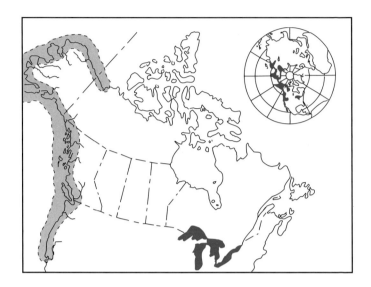

*The Range of Pink Salmon*

originated. Pink salmon have been found spawning in rivers
as far as 400 miles away from their natal stream.

During their biennial runs, as spawning time draws nearer,
the males go through a transformation that is both handsome
and bizarre. They take on a humped back (which explains
the pink's other name, the humpy) and a color of deep pink.

Pink salmon like to spawn near the mouths of rivers. Often, they will venture into estuaries where fresh and saltwater mingle. But young pinks move so quickly (before they are
three inches long) from freshwater to the sea that they are only
rarely seen in most salmon rivers. The pink is a favorite prey
of predatory ocean fish, which perhaps helps keep the pink
salmon population well in balance.

Like the other Pacific salmon, the pink salmon ranges
widely, and can be found in the Pacific and Arctic oceans, the
Bering and Okhotsk seas, and the Sea of Japan. Its North

American range extends from the Sacramento River in California, north to Alaska, including the Aleutian Islands, to the delta of the Mackenzie River. The greatest abundance of fish are to be found in the central part of this range. The northern pink salmon travel a good deal more than their southern cousins, moving freely up and down the Alaskan coast and up to the Bering Strait as far as the coast of Russia. The southern pink salmon keep closer to shore, remaining in the waters from northern California up through Washington.

The peak salt-to-freshwater migrations of pinks occur in July and August. At its peak, a migration can be so large the fish will actually clog the mouths of certain rivers. Among all these fish, it can be difficult to get the attention of an individual fish, but when you do, more often than not, a pink salmon will lash out eagerly at a well-presented fly.

The pink is the smallest of the Pacific Northwest salmon, averaging only about three to four pounds, though some bigger pinks, up to 10 pounds or more, have been caught on occasion. The fly-fishing record is just under 12 pounds. I would call any pink over, say, eight pounds, a trophy fish. Most of the larger pink salmon seem to be caught in the rivers of British Columbia.

As a gamefish, most anglers rank pink salmon as the least sporting of the Pacific salmon, I think this is probably because of their small size and the difficulty of being able to accurately predict the exact time of their dominant biennial spawning run. Compared to the rest of the gamefish species of salmon, sport anglers therefore take only a few pink salmon. Even so, the pink salmon is an aggressive fish, and a lot of fun to fish for with light tackle.

OVERLEAF: *Jim Teeny casting to summer steelhead on the Washougal River in Washington.*

CHAPTER THREE

# THE TEENY TECHNIQUE FOR FLY FISHING FOR STEELHEAD AND SALMON

## APPROACHING AND READING STEELHEAD WATER

### APPROACHING STEELHEAD WATER

I recommend that anglers new to fly fishing for steelhead and salmon* begin their introduction to these fish on a small river. As I've said before, small rivers do not necessarily equal small fish. And it is easier to employ my techniques for steelhead fly fishing on small rivers that provide optimum fishing conditions — the water tends to be clearer so you can see the fish better, and you can wade more easily when you need to, and cover more water. Once you have mastered your approach and search techniques on small rivers and are beginning to un-

---

*For the sake of brevity, and for the balance of this text, except where I make a specific reference to salmon, I will use the word "steelhead" to discuss fly fishing to both species, as the techniques are quite similar.

derstand what stream structures the fish like to hold in, then you can move onto larger or murkier rivers which may require blind casting. On these type waters, your small stream experience will help you in identifying the most likely holding spots for steelhead.

As in trout fishing, the clothing you wear on steelhead water is important and is, in fact, a critical part of your approach to the fish. First, never wear white. Forget about white and remember that bright colors almost always spook steelhead.

Avoid all the neon oranges and bold reds, no matter how popular they are. If you see another angler decked out in these colors, he may look good, but you can smile knowing he's likely not catching many fish. So stick with the darker, more subdued colors, especially for stream and river fishing. Wear bland browns, natural greens, dark blues, clothes that tend to blend with the colors of the river or the habitat you are fishing, colors that will let you blend in as much as possible. The more you blend into your environment, believe me, the closer you'll be able to approach the fish.

Assuming you are not splashing about the water wearing bright clothing, of primary importance in finding fish is studying the water, reading its structures, analyzing its water condition, and getting the feel of it on the particular day you are on the water. Of course, as with all fly fishing, polarized sunglasses are a must. I wear amber-colored ones on cloudy days or on days when the light is real low since they help with glare and provide contrast.

Time of day is also an important consideration when going to the river. I don't agree with a lot of anglers who'll only fish in the early morning or evening. I use the midday sun to my advantage, since I think that when the sun is higher, say from 10:00 A.M. to 4:00 P.M., its rays reduce the glare on the water. And contrary to what other anglers contend, I believe that steelhead bite at midday. I find that steelhead are very active during this time. During the midday hours I also benefit from lower fishing pressure on the water, since many anglers don't fish at that time.

Once you get to the river at the proper time and are wearing the proper attire, put yourself into a position where you can get the best view of fish — up high. This will give you the ability to see more of the river and spot more fish. I sometimes get as high as 25 or 30 feet when I can manage to. Bridges and trees are great observation sites. I find also that it is better to have the sun behind me.

Reading Steelhead Water

One of the keys to successful steelhead fishing is being able to read the different kinds of water and underwater structures where steelhead are likely to be. Moreover, it will help you in being better able to determine the best kind of presentation to make to them. I enjoy angling for steelhead in riffles, runs, pools, pocket water, and tail-outs. Let me explain the characteristics of each of these types of water.

*Riffles* consist of broken, uneven, rapidly moving surface water. Riffles are good holding water for steelhead, because the oxygen level is high and fish feel secure from predators in this type of water. Riffles also work to the angler's advantage, because in such water, since flies tend to drift faster, the fish have less time to decide if the fly passing rapidly by them is artificial or real food. In such water, the steelhead strike is often immediate and fierce. A good pair of polarized glasses and a little patience is all you need to spot fish in a riffle.

When I am talking of *runs*, I mean any stretch of river in which the water has a more or less consistent current flow. Runs are usually deeper water sections below riffles. Uncluttered runs often hold large numbers of steelhead. When working a run or a consistent stretch of water, I think it is best, if possible, to start downstream and work slowly upstream.

Fly fishing for steelhead in the larger, deeper, and slower-moving water of *pools* is much more difficult than fishing in faster water. In fishing a pool, presentation becomes critical. A poor cast, one that slaps the water, for example, will send the fish scurrying. Or if there is sunlight flashing off the pool, you have to be careful even of shadows. Sometimes just the shadow of a line across the water is more than enough to spook steelhead. You have to pay some dues with pool fishing — success requires a good deal of patience.

*Pocket water,* which consists of the more shallow, depressed areas below rapids and long runs, can be deceiving. Despite its name, pocket water is moving water, broken water, often marked by moderate riffles, even small runs of whitewater.

I also like to fish for steelhead in *tail-outs*, which as the name implies, is the area of smooth and calmer water spreading out below the bottom or tail of riffles and pools. It's easy to spot fish in the smooth water of a tail-out.

Of course, when you are scanning the river, be sure to pay attention not just to these favorite holding areas, but to the entire expanse of the river — steelhead can really be anywhere.

## WATER CONDITIONS

### High-Water Conditions

High water brings on different fishing conditions and while high water can be difficult to fish, productive fishing is still possible. You can catch a lot of steelhead in high water. When the water is high and running strong, steelhead like to hang at the slower edges of the current or seams. And when the water is really high, they'll be hanging out near shore, often not more than 10 feet off the bank. Too, during high water, steelhead will hang in tail-outs below riffles and pools. These are great places to fish because you won't need to make long or difficult casts, just short little flips and short little drifts, in close. I've also found that in high-water situations, the fish will often be on the bottom of the water column because of the slower current speed that exists there. In high water, fishing close in toward shore and along the tail-outs will almost always produce fish.

*Low-Water Conditions*

When the water is low, conditions are much more ideal for catching steelhead. In a low-water situation, of course, the fish will be easier to spot. You want to look for fish in the deeper currents where the rivers become more channeled and in protected holding spots. In low-water situations, you will do much better in riffles and pocket water.

## FINDING THE FISH

For the most part, the key to spotting steelhead is to figure out, based upon the observations you have made of the type and condition of the water in the river, where the fish should be resting. (This really helps in blind fishing.) A resting fish is protected from the current and is more likely to strike at your offering. Most of the time, resting steelhead will be close to the bottom where the current is a bit slower. Boulders and slight depressions also provide good resting spots — this holds true in both pocket water and riffles. In faster water, obstructions and depressions are really the only refuges for the fish. Again, look for any place in the watershed where the speed of the current changes from fast to slow.

Where they are holding in fast water, steelhead are more aggressive and therefore much more likely to strike at your offering. Pools and slower water seem to dampen a steelhead's interest in active feeding. While its interest can be piqued, patience and a great deal of determination is called for in fly fishing for the steelhead in slow water, together with a willingness to try different combinations of lines, leaders, flies, casting as well as various presentation techniques.

Also, remember that once you find a good holding spot for a steelhead, the chances are high that this spot will continue to produce for you week after week, and even season after season, provided the water and weather conditions at that spot remain about the same.

As steelhead embark on the return to their native rivers, they are quite different in character from most other trout species, in large  part because, being anadromous fish, they are on a mission to reach a designated spawning area. (It should be noted that spring/summer-run steelhead have the same instincts and habits as their winter counterparts, though as I mentioned before, they are not as much in a hurry since their spawning season is months away.)

Steelhead are extremely shy and wary as they enter the rivers, and they are, for trout, unexpectedly selective about their movements. A principal difference between trout and steelhead is that trout tend to stay in one area of a river for their entire lives, whereas steelhead are constantly on the move throughout the entire watershed. Depending upon water temperatures and levels, steelhead prefer to hold close to the banks, at the edge of hard currents, and in drift water, which allows them to get away from hard, rushing water. They will move quickly through whitewater, delighting in the heavy levels of oxygen generated by moving water.

Of course, high ocean tides will bring more fish in, because it becomes easier for steelhead to travel in the increased water flow of a high tide. But even on a low tide, when the water is lower and slower moving, or on a slack tide when there is no movement of water at all, steelhead will enter freshwater streams. When their urge to spawn is strong enough, steelhead will even swim in very shallow riffles and runs with their backs exposed above the surface of the water.

## LOW-PRESSURE/HIGH-PRESSURE STEELHEAD

Steelhead that have not been fished for a time, fish holding in undisturbed water, are what I call low-pressure fish. Wary, but still calm, these low-pressure fish are easier to spot than steelhead that have been fished over frequently and have become nervous and spooky. With an accurate and smooth presentation, you can often take such low-pressure fish on the first cast. Indeed, these low pressure fish can often even be tempted to the surface to strike.

Unfortunately — at least in the steelhead rivers of the Pacific Northwest — anglers only rarely find low-pressure steelhead, at least in any numbers. This is probably because from winter through summer, our steelhead runs are being fished consistently, and as a consequence fishing becomes increasingly difficult throughout the year.

This predominance of high-pressure fish in the waters of the Pacific Northwest is one of the principal reasons why I think it is most productive to fly fish for them with sinking lines and sinking flies. After entering the rivers, most of our steelhead will only rarely come to the surface. The only way to tempt them is to get the fly down to where they are in the water column, whether it be in whitewater, riffles, pocket water, pools, or tail-outs.


## THE ADVANTAGES OF SIGHT FISHING

I almost exclusively sight fish. Everyone knows that I'm fond of saying "If I spot 'em, I've got 'em." I believe that if I can see the fish, my chances of hooking it are 75 to 80 percent.

Sight fishing allows me to watch the fish closely, monitoring its behavior, even following it if I have to in order to improve my chances for a better presentation. Becoming good at spotting fish takes a lot of practice, patience, and most of all *concentration*. It is particularly difficult on windy days or in areas with surface current, since both conditions tend to conceal fish. Sometimes you can see the entire fish, but it is more likely that you will spot only some part of it first — a moving tail, a flash of movement, a mouth opening or closing. If you think that you've spotted a good fish, move as close as you can to it without spooking it, careful to keep your eye on the fish. If you're at a distance and can't get any closer, you might try using a pair of binoculars. Once you have spotted a good fish, or know where the fish should be holding, you can position yourself properly in relation to it and begin your presentations. So, locating the fish, bar none, is the biggest advantage you are going to have in this type fishing.

The trick to spotting steelhead in moving water is to really concentrate, taking your time to steadily go over the water. We all have a tendency to look over water too quickly, I think. You've got to penetrate underneath the surface and down to the bottom *visually*, trying to capture in your mind's eye a form or something that you think might be a fish. After you spend a little time concentrating, you'll find that all of the sudden a smooth slick will move into your line of vision — this is something I call a "window" — at which point you can see *everything*. The window in the water won't last long, maybe just a second or two, and then it will disappear. But if you'll wait, another window will appear and you'll be able to verify whether or not there is a fish or even several fish in the particular area of the river you are concentrating on.

Believe me, I have fished to a lot of things that weren't really fish. It doesn't usually happen on the rivers that I fish often, since at this point I know all of the rocks and obstructions in these rivers and don't usually mistake a rock or a log for a fish. But in new and strange water, I have actually gone on point to a long, gray rock, figuring it was a nice steelhead. But it wasn't at all. Until I discovered my mistake, I stayed on that rock like a bird dog. And I cast to it from where I was. In these type situations, I don't move out of position. A lot of anglers will go upstream to make a cast that will give them a better swing of the fly. Not me. I don't move out of position. I like to keep that potential fish in my sights. I stay right where I am and make my cast. Then, if I don't get any response, I may move forward slowly until I can get close enough to really distinguish whether or not my target is a fish. Also, the closer I get, the better I can follow my fly in order to track it, which helps me considerably with my presentation.

I have had more guys come up behind me when I am fishing and say "Oh, there's nothing here, let's go!" and they'll move on. But I'll be looking at three or four steelhead in that spot. Now, I'm not going to try to change their minds!

### Advice For Blind Fishing

If conditions are such (the river is big or the water is murky) that you will not be able to actually see the fish, then you will have to fish by reading the water and by studying the river, figuring out where the fish are likely to be holding. As I mentioned previously, if the river is up and running hard, the steelhead will be hanging close to the banks, in the riffles, in the pocket water, and in tail-outs.

Much like steelhead, salmon like large pools and cut banks. They can also be found hanging in deep currents and eddies, water that steelhead shy away from. Patience and persistence pay off. Experience pays off. Those are two angling cliches that still hold true. And if you are a novice and are for the first time fishing difficult water in which you are unable to see the fish, then, if possible, watch as many other steelhead and salmon fly fishermen as you can, study everything they do, learn and apply their technique to your game.

Whether you are angling for steelhead or salmon, always look for those stretches of water that provide cover. During the early mornings and late afternoons, steelhead that haven't been under a lot of angling pressure can be found in tail-outs

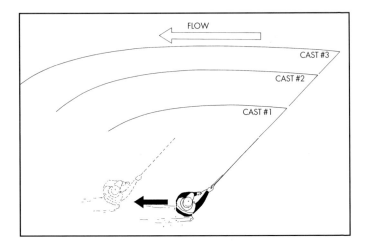

*Jim's Presentation for Blind Fishing*

below rapids, in the calm water above rock ledges, on the backside and in front of individual or galleries of boulders. When I'm fishing the mornings and early afternoons for steelhead, I like to fish the tail-outs first. If steelhead are there, then I will settle down and fish the entire run. I cover the water very carefully and entirely.

To best do this, I cast upstream for a deep drift, allowing the fly to swing back towards me until it is directly below me. I will repeat this exercise, this time lengthening the cast farther out about two feet. I will continue the exercise, each time expanding the cast about two feet until I am confident that I have completely covered what I consider to be the good water. If I get no results, I move downstream and repeat the procedure all over again.

### "ROCKING" STEELHEAD

One particular (and controversial) technique that I have been noted for is "rocking" fish. If I find a steelhead in a place where for whatever reason — maybe there is some kind of obstruction, a boulder, or a downed tree in my way — I am unable to make a decent presentation and get the fly close to the fish, if I absolutely have no other choice, I will throw a rock near the fish to move it to a place in the river that is more advantageous for me. This would preferably be a more open spot where I can see the fish better and get a better drift of my fly, either upstream or downstream. I find it easier to move steelhead from a shallow spot to a deeper place, because I believe the fish feels more protected in the deeper water. To entice the fish to move upstream, I'll throw the rock below it; to move downstream, I'll throw the rock above it — creating just a small amount of disturbance to get the fish going. Let me make it clear that I'm not trying to hurt the fish. I'm not throwing the rock directly at it. And, I will always ask any other anglers on the stream if they mind if I throw a few rocks.

I also use the rocking technique when I am confronted with steelhead who are really lethargic and not getting excited by the sight of my fly. In these situations, I find that if I get the fish moving, they seem to become re-energized and more excited about going for my fly.

## CASTING AND PRESENTATIONS

Presentation. It's a word, a subject, I talk about often, and really, its importance to successful fly fishing, whether it be for brown trout or steelhead, cannot be over-emphasized. The perfect fly selection, the perfect rod, the perfect balance of line, leader, and tippet, all mean nothing without a smooth and accurate presentation.

For really productive steelhead and salmon fishing, you simply must get your fly under the water and down in the water column to where the fish are holding, so your selection of a fly line is critical (as I'll be discussing in more detail later). I am not saying that you should consistently fish right on the bottom; indeed, you will have better luck if you stay somewhat above the bottom, or simply bounce your fly off the bottom.

After I've spotted my fish, I get as close to it as possible for the best presentation position, insuring greater accuracy in my casting and offering me more control. Usually the best presentation should be made slightly downstream from the position of the fish so that it can't see you and so that you can more easily obtain a drag-free, dead-drift presentation. But the most important thing is to try to keep in sight of that fish, even if it means adjusting your cast or using a cast you'd rather not use — say, a roll cast rather than a full back cast.

Adjust your position as the situation warrants, moving a little downstream, perhaps, or a few feet upstream. Remember that every movement modifies your presentation and you have to be able to make the necessary adjustments as you move. And you will surely have to move. Rarely are any steelhead caught from one position. Fly fishermen spend as much time jockeying around for the best position as they do actually casting. And often, it is this constant shifting about for the right angle, the right position, that will finally move the fish and get it to strike. Remember, as you're getting into position, be sure to be very quiet. These fish are extremely spooky.

Getting into a good position to make your presentation, either to a sighted fish or a good stretch of steelhead water — a run, pool, riffle, boulder, whatever — is actually an essential part of a successful presentation. Good position, plus a good cast, only increase your chances of hooking a fish.

Study the water you plan to fish carefully. Don't rush things; if you can't see the fish, decide where you think they should be holding. Plan your cast, especially that all important first one, in as much detail as you can. Consider details like the current, slack, drift, and desired sink rate of your fly. Taking all of these factors into consideration before you begin casting will improve your chances of a quick strike. If a strike doesn't come quickly, continue to observe and take into account everything you are doing, every facet of the conditions around you, and adjust your presentation accordingly.

When casting to steelhead, I use a roll cast about 80 percent of the time. It's very useful on small streams with a lot of obstructions to the rear that would make an ordinary back cast difficult. And if I execute it properly, it's a much faster cast for me than, say, an overhead cast. And if I've spotted a fish, the faster I can get my fly into the water the better!

For my roll cast, starting with my rod tip lower than normal, or near the surface, I'll strip a lot of line out so that I have an ample amount of line weight outside my rod tip. Then I take the rod back and up until the rod is behind my shoulder at about the two o'clock position. After I have allowed the line to come to a slight stop on the surface of the water, I'll flip my rod forward (my rod will be pointed towards my target), making a normal forward cast. Remember to keep the rod tip level with the surface — it shouldn't be held too high — this will help give you a bit more distance (about five or 10 feet) without exerting too much energy.

Lefty covers roll casting much more extensively in his books in the Library, *Lefty Kreh's Modern Fly Casting Method* and *Advanced Fly Casting*, so review these two volumes for more details on the roll cast. Keep in mind that the roll cast technique that I have described is one for use with a floating line. When roll casting with a sink-tip or full-sinking line, a single or double water haul should be used.

Now comes the hard part, estimating how far upstream you'll have to cast your fly line in order to get that fly to drift naturally into the steelhead's strike zone. What I'll usually do is select some sort of target upstream of the fish's position to

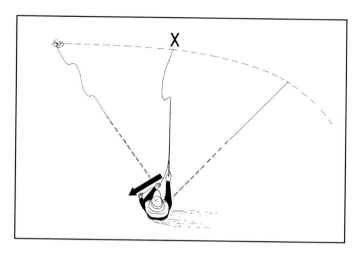

*Stripping in Slack*

serve as my aiming point — a rock, a boulder, or whatever. Be sure to cast well above the fish so that you don't spook it. Continue to make casts, varying them until you've got that fly right where you want it to land.

Before you begin your retrieve on any cast, be sure that you allow the fly to sink fully. This is where a lot of fly fishermen make a big mistake on steelhead: they start their retrieve too soon. Remember, you've got to give your fly the time to get right in front of the fish's nose — it's generally not going to rise to it.

Your presentation should be a dead-drift of the fly, moving only with the flow of the current, avoiding any kind of unnatural drag. Most of the time, it is natural movement of the fly that will induce the steelhead to strike. After casting upstream, when that fly line starts to come back towards you, strip any slack in so that the fly continues to drift naturally with the current. Keep the line tight so that you can feel the take. A steelhead's take can be extremely subtle. With this presentation, it's important to keep your rod tip low, parallel and close to the water. The low rod position provides you with more sensitivity to your fly line.

Be sure also to watch the fish, because — particularly in a slow-water situation — sometimes you can see it take the fly before you can actually feel it on the line. When you feel that take, set the hook quickly and follow the techniques for setting the hook, fighting, landing, and releasing the fish that I will be discussing later in the book.

Also, when you see that fish coming to take your fly, don't stop your retrieve. Out of excitement, I suppose, a lot of anglers tend to stop their retrieve. This will totally turn off that fish! Play it through. Sometimes you have to gamble, but, again, you'll have to experiment a little bit.

If you don't get a strike after several presentations, the light bulb should go off in your head, telling you that something in your tactics is not on the mark. At this point, change your presentation — the color or size of the fly; or the angle of your presentation — move upstream or downstream; or, even try giving your fly a little action. Above all, don't give up. If you haven't spooked the fish and it's still in your view, continue to put that fly in front of the fish's nose. And I want to repeat what I said earlier, because it is very important: *make sure that you are giving your fly sufficient time to reach the proper position just in front of the fish.* I see anglers making this mistake all of the time, picking up their fly and re-casting too soon. Patience usually pays off.

Once, while fishing a pool on the Sandy River, I simply could not get the fish to strike. Everything scared them — conventional and fly-fishing tackle. I mean everything. I was determined to find some method of getting the fly to them without spooking them first. Finally, believing that the fish were not really on the bottom, but hanging somewhere up higher in the water column, I switched to a sink-tip line, long leader, and a smaller fly. Eventually, I ended up with a rig consisting of a 14-foot leader, a 4-pound tippet, and various small Teeny Nymphs, in black, insect green, natural, and antique gold dressings. Before the afternoon had given way to dusk, I hooked 11 steelhead from that exasperating pool. Five of them were really nice fish, weighing over 14 pounds. Making a similar change in technique or tackle has given me success with steelhead in a great many previously difficult angling situations, during winter, spring, and summer runs. It absolutely opened up a whole new world for me.

As I've said over and over, being able to see the fish truly is an advantage when you are fishing for steelhead and salmon. Also, seeing the fish, being able to observe and study them, adds a great deal of pure enjoyment to the fishing. Keeping a fish in sight while you fish it lets you know what you are doing right and what you are doing wrong. If your presentation is off, the fish will vanish and you will know immediately what you've done wrong and how to correct it next time.

Sight fishing requires extreme patience and discipline, but the rewards are more than worth the caution, and sight fishing will quickly hone your fly-fishing skills. When I am on a good trophy fish, I try to stay with it (if I don't scare it off), adjusting my cast, changing leaders, tippet, fly — whatever it takes to get the fish's interest and make it strike. Oftentimes, persistence is even more important than pure angling skill. By keeping the fish in sight, you can study its behavior, its movements, you can see at once how it reacts (or fails to react) to your fly. You can determine if you are putting the fly too far away, too deep, or too shallow. Also, by keeping the fish in sight, you don't have to wait for the feel of the strike, you can often actually watch it take the fly, and simply set the hook as it closes its mouth.

Take your time on steelhead! I like to take my time, collecting myself, watching the speed of the current and how everything drifts, before I make my first cast. I look for things in the water like leaves or sticks and follow them as they drift along. This will give me a true feel for the water flow. Then I'll pick a target and say to myself, for example, "I've got to cast to that boulder in order to get that fly to be down right there when it hits the water, and with this current speed, that's about eight feet away," and so on.

If my first and later casts don't spook the fish, if it remains a good holding fish and I can still see it, I may spend as much as an hour or more on that one fish. Again, take your time with steelhead . . . patience pays off.

### PRESENTATIONS TO WINTER AND SPRING/SUMMER STEELHEAD

Some anglers insist that winter and spring/summer steelhead require different presentation techniques and tackle. That may be true to a certain extent. I agree that the difference in the water temperature from one season to another does require some adaptation of your presentation. But overall, as far as I am concerned, a steelhead is a steelhead, and if given the same conditions (either in winter or spring/summer) I'll use the same approach.

In the summer when the rivers are usually lower and clearer, it is easier to read the water and wade safely into different areas. Oftentimes, on smaller rivers, you can even wade across the entire river, working all the little pockets, giving you the advantage of being able to cover more water.

Unlike some anglers, I never switch to lighter tackle in the summer. I never use a leader or tippet below 8-pound test for steelhead at any time, whether in fast or slow water. Occasionally, if the situation requires, I might have to switch from my usual full-sinking line to a floating line or a sink-tip line. Again, you never know, you always have to be prepared to adapt to any situation that you might encounter.

Also, in the summer, as a rule I rarely switch to smaller fly patterns. I normally prefer to fish flies in hook sizes #2 - #6. I will only drop down to #8 or #10 if I absolutely have to. I don't think dropping down to small flies is really necessary unless you're in a situation where the water is low and clear, such as in a smaller stream, or when you feel that the fish are being extremely spooky.

In this type situation, the big, bold attractor patterns that work so well in the winter won't usually draw a strike. In low, clear water situations if you cast a big fly into the water, it will generally scare the fish to death, so, your approach on spring/summer-run fish needs to be more discreet. In summer, I usually have more consistent action with the darker colors — black, green, antique gold, natural, and purple.

Because winter creates colder water temperatures, you need to slow down the movement of your fly, getting it a little deeper in the water column. This generally calls for the use of a sinking fly line or shooting-taper that will get the fly down to the fish more consistently. In cold weather, the fish have less of a tendency to move in order to chase the fly, and their strike zone becomes smaller. So again — particularly for winter-run fish — that means that you simply have to put your fly right in front of their noses. It has been my experience that winter-run steelhead are much more spooky about being approached by anglers than spring/summer fish. I don't have a scientific explanation for this, but winter steelhead seem to move away a lot faster as you approach them, moving to a sanctuary or even completely out of the area. But I've had spring/summer-run fish allow me to walk right up to them as close as a rod's length away. These spring/summer fish don't seem to have the fear of humans that is so characteristic of winter-run fish. It may have something to do with the fact that the spring/sum-

*Float fishing for Pacific salmon in Alaska.* ➤

mer-run fish spend more time in freshwater before spawning, sometimes eight or nine months, and perhaps over this long period of time they have become accustomed to having anglers sharing their water.

Also, in winter, usually on the average you are not going to be able to spot fish as easily. In cold water, the fish won't be moving as much, and you'll be encountering more low light and low visibility (color in the water) situations then. So you have to be able to read the water, understand it, and fish it with normal wet-fly drift-fishing techniques. Here your skills of reading the water and figuring out where the steelhead are holding will come into play. Though I do find that there are quite a few days in the winter when the water warms up above 40 degrees Fahrenheit, and the action can get really good. Also, I sometimes find that after a good hard freeze the night before, a river drops and clears in a hurry and you can have incredibly crystal clear water conditions.

### PRESENTATIONS IN VARIOUS TYPES OF WATER

*Pools*

Deep slow-water pools are a good starting point for practicing all the essential elements of the good presentation that I have been discussing. Deep pools provide an easy current and good holding spots for steelhead, especially if there is heavy fishing pressure on the river or water conditions are such that the fish are having difficulty traveling upstream. In fact, it is not unusual for steelhead to stay in pools for a long time.

But steelhead are much more spooky in slow water than they are in fast water. This means that fishing in slow-water conditions requires a great deal of patience. You'll make a lot of casts — sometimes as many as 50 to one fish! — and do a lot of experimentation with your outfit, your fly patterns, and your angles of presentation. Because you can see the fish, sometimes it may very well be able to see you. It will certainly have ample opportunity to closely examine your fly. So just as in trout fishing, the key to fly fishing for steelhead in slow water is to make a good, totally natural presentation. And there's no getting around it: to make a good presentation in these circumstances is going to require a certain degree of skill on your part.

So let's go on to technique. In a slow, deep-water situation, I'm first going to arm myself with a fast-sinking line and a short leader (3 or 4 feet). Generally speaking, a deep-water situation presents two aspects that must be taken into account by the angler: how deep is the water, and how fast is the speed of the current. Usually, in a normal deep-water situation, I'll start out with a very fast-sinking line, such as one of my T-Series lines, a T-400 or T-500. (And I trust the reader will forgive me for plugging my own products in this book, but these are really the only fly lines I fish with and know the most about.) Incidentally, I'll start fishing with these same lines in fast water if the steelhead are three or four feet deep. The key is to get the fly to the right level and oftentimes lighter or slower sinking lines are not able to accomplish that quickly.

So, say I start out with the T-400, and I spot a fish and start casting to it. If I find that I snag up a little bit too quickly or miss the fish because the fly is sinking and traveling too rapidly, I then switch to the T-300, which is 100 grains lighter than the T-400. Conversely, if I am using the T-400 and having trouble getting the fly down close to the fish, I then switch to the heavier T-500 line. *This ability (and willingness) to switch line weights and adapt your technique to different circumstances and situations is a critical success factor in steelhead fishing.*

In some situations, I can accomplish the same goal without having to take the time to switch lines, simply by lengthening or shortening the length of line I cast. For example, if I am fishing the T-400 line and it isn't getting my fly down to the fish, I simply cast more line farther upstream than I normally would. This buys me a few extra seconds of drift time for the line to sink to the desired lower depth in the water column. Or, if I'm casting a T-400 line that is sinking too quickly to satisfy me, I can simply shorten my upstream cast so that the line has less time to sink and will be traveling at a higher position in the water column.

When you've spotted a steelhead, *keep an eye on it the entire time you are making your presentation.* After all, you've gone to a lot of trouble locating that fish, and you don't want to lose it by making a casual glance away while you're loading your rod or talking to your buddy. Oftentimes in a pool situation, after you have thrown a few casts — either hooking fish or not — the fish is going to move up or downstream into pocket water for protection, and you want to be able to follow it.

### Runs

Fishing runs can be a lot of fun. Again, a run is a long consistent piece of water. A drift can also be called a run — swift flowing water or riffling water going along with great consistency. Even if it contains a submerged boulder or two, such water should still be classified as a run. In the summer (and even sometimes in the winter on certain rivers), runs offer a chance for clear, unobstructed steelhead sighting. And you know that if you can figure out where the fish are holding in a run, you have an excellent chance for making a good accurate presentation since you know exactly where to place your fly line and fly.

Normally, when fishing a run I will begin at its tail-out — the lower end of the run before it spills off into rapids or into whitewater to go into another drift. Then after a while, if I've hooked some fish, great, I'll stay there. If not, I'll figure that I have spooked some of the fish and that they have moved up into the head of the run. Usually the fish that were originally holding in the lower end of a run that were not caught or hooked will now be concentrated in the middle or upper end, depending on the conformation of the stream bed. So, I'll begin to move towards the head of that run.

What is nice about fishing a run is that usually you are able to make a good quarter-cast upstream or straight across, allowing the fly to sink, dead drift, and swing through — employing normal wet fly-fishing techniques. This is really not high-tech, state-of-the-art fly fishing. It is simply being able to cast your fly line out properly, letting it sink and swing. You can get a hook-up at any point of the swing and drift of the fly. The entire presentation — almost from the beginning to the end — offers you the potential for fish to take your fly. Especially if they're not too spooky, steelhead will generally strike on the swing or during the tail-end of your drift, or even sometimes just as you are picking up your fly for another cast.

An alternative technique in this type of fishing is to strip in line just once or twice during the drift to make the fly move a foot or so, and then hold it for just a split second. If that does not draw a strike, then try stripping the line in very quickly, re-cast, and go through the drift routine again.

Fishing in runs gives you many opportunities for success. If you haven't been able to get fish at the tail-end or the head of the run, you may very well find fish in the middle of the run where the water is usually deeper and offers steelhead more oxygen and a little more protection.

Normally, on days when we are really hooking big numbers of fish, it usually happens in a run.

### Pocket Water and Riffles

While steelhead may never be easy fish to catch, contrary to most anglers, I find that they are easier to work in pocket water and riffles than in any other kind of water. During their spawning runs, it is not uncommon for steelhead to school in large sections of pocket water. And, if the river is experiencing heavy fishing pressure, I have found that pocket water and riffles are the spots steelhead will go to avoid anglers. In fact, I would say that under heavy fishing pressure, fishing pocket water is the best way to get steelhead. Again, in pocket water and riffles, there are obstructions and depressions that break up the speed of the current and provide safe havens for the fish.

Most anglers don't like to fish pocket water, because it's tricky. Though, I think it's easier because I feel that the fish is more likely to a make mistake, i.e. go after my fly, in this type water. I think a fish also has a heightened sense of security in pocket water because there is more cover available to it. Moreover, it doesn't have the luxury of time in the fast pocket water to closely examine — and possibly reject — an artificial fly. And of course this kind of fishing is fun — fast and furious! Pocket-water steelhead are much more aggressive and always seem to be much more tuned in to taking something.

When fishing fast pocket water, getting the fly down into the water quickly is critical. For this fishing, I like to use a floating line to accomplish that purpose. Unlike a full-sinking line or a shooting-taper, the floating line enables you to adapt better to the characteristics of pocket water — the faster, bouldery-type, broken water. You'll find that it won't be necessary to cast great distances. You can cast shorter, closer, more precise casts. Also, the floating line provides more control for accurate placement of the fly on the water, and is easy to mend to maintain drag-free drifts.

When using a standard floating line, in order to get the fly down really fast, I sometimes add a piece of split-shot to a short 7-foot leader. (Note, however, that the use of split-shot is an illegal practice on some watersheds, so make sure you are familiar with the current fishing regulations of whatever water you are fishing.) Split-shot will really get the fly down deep among the boulders where steelhead often hold. What size

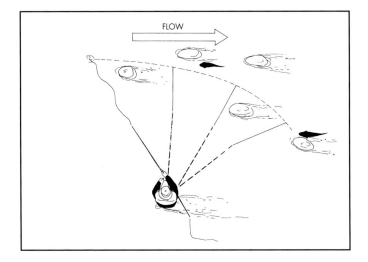

*Lob Cast*

shot to use is dependent upon the water current, the depth you're trying to reach, and how the pocket water is affecting the current flow. I rig split-shot on the leader above the tippet, about 24 inches away from my fly.

The weight of the split-shot is obviously going to affect your cast, so you have to work with it, get it right, get it so that after a couple of false casts, you can work the heavier rig smoothly and be able to place your fly exactly where you want it to go. On most pocket water, average casts will go no farther than from 15 to perhaps 30 feet. But because these are short casts, they need to be accurate, dead on.

When I add weight to the fly line, I find that getting the fly to the fish with a conventional cast is difficult. I call this type of short-line work "combat casting," because sometimes it is hard to maintain balance and accuracy. For this presentation, I use something I call a "lob cast." I'll start the cast by stripping off some line. Then I'll take my rod back beyond my shoulder to a two o'clock position and cast forward (like an overhead throwing action), pointing the rod tip towards the target with one continuous and fluid movement. What I am actually doing is lobbing my fly line through the rod guides towards the target. The cast is usually made under 30 feet, so that while distance is not that important, accuracy is.

As soon as the split-shot hits the water, I direct the line through the current flow with my fly rod, hopefully bringing the fly right in front of the steelhead's nose. An extra benefit with this presentation is that it minimizes snags or hang-ups, an ever-present problem with the rocks and boulders that surround pocket water.

The downside of pocket fishing is that you don't always land your fish. It's really difficult to play a fish in this type water which is generally full of boulders and fallen wood obstructions. Remember to keep your rod high and your line tight after the hook-up. Most importantly, keep your eye on that fish and be prepared to follow it if it moves away.

When fishing pocket water as well as pools, remember — especially if you can see the fish — that a delicate presentation is necessary, as is a slow retrieve, even a dead drift, letting the current work the fly. Concentration is just as important, because sometimes the strike will be soft, delicate, an uncharacteristic gentle twitch or tug. So you've got to keep an eye on the leader and a finger on the line. If the fish are visible, when a steelhead begins to strike, you should be able to see its distinctive open, white mouth. Set the hook hard just as its mouth closes or when you can see its head turn suddenly.

Presentation, that is, making an accurate cast and fishing the fly at the right depth, is essential to fishing fast runs productively. The key is to get the fly down to the fish so that it can see it. Make a false cast and then cast. Watch your line and fly drift through the current. Continue to do this with different variations, maybe moving farther up or downstream.

If you continue to get snag-ups, try making a shorter cast. You have to put all of these pieces together to complete the puzzle.

## LINE CONTROL

With steelhead and salmon fishing, line control is essential. Here's how I recommend doing it.

Once you have made your cast and you're satisfied with your presentation and the lay of your line, lower your rod to release tension from the line. Bring the rod tip down almost level with, or just slightly below, the level of your line. Holding the rod in this manner will increase the sensitivity of the rod tip and if a fish does strike, you'll feel the strike instantly. Whereas, if you have the rod tip pointing upward, so that there is a big bend or belly of line hanging down, you may miss the strike because you won't feel it along the line as quickly.

I control my fly line with my first two fingers — keeping my thumb on the top of the rod and allowing the line to run

*Line Control*

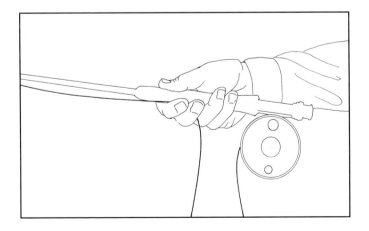

through my fingers. The fingers act like another ferrule, one that feels for the strike. That way, I can just hold the line and let it drift when needed. The sensitivity of my fingers allows me to feel a little hit or slight hesitation so that I can immediately set the hook.

Always being in direct contact with the line in this manner also allows for better control, letting you quickly adjust for slack, or to mend or pick up line.

With steelhead, you don't want to keep a really tight line. After your initial cast, mend the line, let it go slightly soft, applying little, if any, tension. You will still be able to feel the strike and set the hook in plenty of time. Any irregular movement of the line, a slight grab or twitch, will signal the strike. Then you should allow a nearly imperceptible pause to occur and really set the hook hard.


## THE STRIKE AND SETTING THE HOOK

I have had many opportunities to watch the habits of steelhead. I think that steelhead do have strike zones, but they may not be as specific as those of trout. I do know that steelhead are curious and territorial, which is something an angler can use to his advantage. If you can make your fly come closer to the fish, you're going to get more strikes, more consistently.

I've also been in situations where I've hooked a steelhead, fought it, and then lost it. Now, that particular fish may or may not go back to its same holding spot. But I've come back a day or two later and seen it right back there in the same exact spot where I hooked it before. So that tells me that steelhead are territorial, they will go back to a specific lie, and that area is obviously going to be good holding water for other steelhead in the river. So, as a particular fish moves on, usually you'll find that another steelhead will move into that same holding spot.

Water temperature plays a big part in striking. As the water gets colder, the fish don't have the tendency to chase the fly nearly as far. In the spring and summer, because the water is a little warmer, the fish will be more aggressive towards the fly. Oftentimes, they will even come to the surface for a take. Whereas in the winter, it would be rare for you to get a steelhead to come up and take a surface fly.

Clarity also plays a role because the fish can't move for something they can't see. When fishing for winter-run steelhead in cloudy or off-color water (or if you encounter this situation in the summer), your number one goal should be to try to get the fly down as deep as possible and as close as possible to where you think the steelhead are actually holding. This will be your best chance to get the fish.

A steelhead's strike can be very deceptive. It can be difficult to judge, even by the best steelhead anglers. Missing steelhead on the strike is common. Believe me, even with my experience, I still miss fish. Only persistence, practice, and experience will improve your ability in picking up strikes and setting the hook.

Sometimes with steelhead, I don't think I really ever feel anything. The strike just becomes something you sense and then the rest is all instinct. If you think you have a strike, think you sense it, then by all means go for it, set the hook and set it as though the fish had hit your fly violently. More often than not, a sensed strike on steelhead turns out to be a true strike. And if not, even if your false strike turns out to be only a stick, grass, or a rock, at least you're learning how different things feel against your line.

I can't tell you how many times, just because I thought there might possibly be a fish there, I lifted up my rod and started to tighten the line and discovered there really was a fish there. I'm not saying that I do it with any great consistency, but once in a while, I can really sense it.

After the strike is perceived, there are several options for setting the hook. Some anglers believe lifting the rod tip straight up is the proper way of setting the hook; others believe in yanking the rod either to the left or to the right. In fishing for steelhead and salmon, any of these methods should work.

Because I am right-handed, when I get a strike, I tend to set the hook by driving the rod, in one fluid motion, both up and to the right. It's a natural movement for me and seems to work well, so I have not fiddled with it. That is the way I set the hook when I'm fishing either steelhead and salmon.

The sideways hook, either to the left or to the right, is probably the most popular method of setting the hook on steelhead and salmon. Setting the hook sideways is called "setting the hook in the hinge." The only problem with this method is that against a fish that has sharp teeth, sometimes the leader will cross the jaw and the teeth, severing the leader.

Also, I set the hook hard and sure. After working so hard at finding fish, setting yourself up, and making the right presentation, it would be a real misery to lose it by not setting the hook hard enough. So don't be afraid to put some muscle into it, especially when fishing bigger steelhead and salmon, because once they are hooked they can be fierce fighters and will thrash about quite a bit, often dislodging a weak hook-set.

## FIGHTING AND LANDING THE FISH

Once you've hooked a steelhead or salmon, it is important that you keep tension on the fish by keeping the tip of the rod lifted, which maintains a steady resistance against the fish. Indeed, by lifting the rod and rod tip you are actually trying to move the fish, taking the advantage away from it. It is this constant pressure of the line on fish that makes them jump, thrash, and run for deep water.

When the fish has stopped running and is hanging in deep water — say a tail-out — but still has a good deal of fight left in it, you can drop the rod slightly so that it is parallel to the water, either to the left or right, with the tip held slightly up. This position, which is similar to the one I use for setting the hook, should work well to keep pressure on the tiring fish without giving it too much slack.

You can then increase the pressure on the fish by simply walking backwards. Called "walking a fish," this technique is an extremely effective way of working tiring steelhead and salmon. Naturally, as you walk a fish, you are gaining line on it, always putting line on the reel, taking up the slack. Walking fish works especially well once a fish has gotten into a drift or tail-out, or when a fish has run into a fast current or whitewater and has begun to tire. You are actually pulling the fish along and it's not feeling the lifting pressure, so you will get less resistance from it. I have saved many fish doing this. Of course, you shouldn't use this technique on a fish that's still fighting and headed downstream.

Basically, my strategy for big fish applies to almost any species of fish, be it big steelhead, salmon, big trout, or tarpon. I've learned a lot from Lefty and, especially, Billy Pate, about fighting tarpon. Their saltwater tactics work very well for me when I'm fighting a big salmon. Once you've hooked a big fish, you simply cannot have any slack. You've got to keep constant tension on the line. This is especially true these days, when so many of the salmon watersheds are requiring anglers to use single, barbless hooks.

With big fish, pumping the rod, smoothing, taking line on the downside of the rod arc, is a wise tactic and one that produces consistent results while keeping a constant degree of resistance against the fish, no matter what it is doing.

In addition to pumping the rod, you can, as the situation warrants, change the angle of the rod, especially the rod tip.

If you are pulling straight up, vary the angle of your rod by making a sideways haul, working the fish both from the left and the right. Work all the angles. As long as you're applying pressure, you are tiring the fish.

Indeed, oftentimes when I have a fish that has gone through several runs and is still at a long distance from me — hanging in a drop-off, behind a boulder, under a log, or in a run of whitewater just teetering, moving back and forth, building up its energy — I will drop my rod tip so that it is just above the water and I will hold the reel tight. This increases the pressure on the fish, preventing it from restoring its energy. Then I simply begin walking rod, reel, and fish backwards, usually towards the shoreline. As I mentioned before, often you can walk an exhausted fish out of difficult water, back into the drift of the main channel, and even begin to haul it toward the bank.

Before steelhead or salmon begin to tire, however, you have to fight them hard. Both are very fast fish, violent fighters, and you have to be able to match their speed, move for move, altering the angle of the rod to frustrate whatever movements they are trying to make to escape, always keeping the pressure and tension constant. The idea is not to give them a moment to rest, to keep them off balance. Every time these fish give an inch, make sure you put that inch on the reel. Don't be afraid to pump the rod, reeling in on the bend you have placed in the rod. Likewise, when a fish wants to run, don't fight it, let it run, then begin pumping again, picking up the line you've given it, plus any more it will let you have.

Some anglers like to throw slack to fighting fish. While this technique has some advantages, especially with big saltwater fish, I almost never use it when I am fishing steelhead and salmon. I believe that giving slack to these fish only increases the chances of them breaking off, of losing them altogether. Instead, I advocate constant pressure that will usually exhaust even big steelhead or salmon quickly.

This is one reason why I use heavy leaders (usually 12, 15, or 20-pound test) when I'm fishing steelhead and salmon. Heavy leaders give you greater control when fighting fish, allowing you to keep the pressure on without worrying about breaking the leader and losing the fish. Heavy leaders really let you go after the fish, bringing them in quickly so that you can release them in much better shape than they would be in after a very long fight on a light leader.

While you should keep constant pressure on the fish, many anglers have a tendency to apply more pressure at the end of the fight. I think people rush and push too hard at this stage, because it is one of the most exciting times, particularly if you've got a trophy on the line. Remember, don't push it!

Also, when fighting steelhead and salmon, usually you should try, if you can, to stay slightly upstream of the fish. But if you hook into a really big fish, you will find it is easier to fight it from below, from the downstream side. That way you have the fish upstream, trying to fight both you and the current. This double struggle will normally exhaust even the biggest fish quickly. To repeat, if it's a modestly sized fish under normal circumstances, say a long, uncomplicated run of water, then try and take it from above; otherwise, the critical fighting position that you should take is from below the fish.

No matter how you fight a hooked and running steelhead or salmon, whenever possible try and get out of the water and fight it from the bank, or at least from the shallow edges. Once you've had a strike, see if you cannot back the fish up so you can get out of the water. It's a good strategy to use on steelhead and salmon, because it will tend to reduce their runs and keep them closer to shore. When you back up in this manner, this puts the fish at a big disadvantage. Because the fish is now in shallow water, it is out of the current, has less oxygen available to it, and won't be able to fight as well. Being out of the water also gives you a lot more control over any unexpected situation that may arise, and will let you adjust much more quickly to whatever unexpected movement the fish might make. If the fish goes upstream or downstream, for example, you're better able to go with it. You can also turn more quickly and not have to worry about slipping in the water.

Many anglers let excitement get the best of them once they have fought a big salmon or steelhead to exhaustion. Seeing the fish is spent, they will let off, ease off, thinking the battle is over. This is a mistake. A big fish can break off at any time, even after it has gone over onto its side and is drifting in shallow water. It's when you have hauled the fish this close that your leader and tippet are at their weakest. You have to keep the pressure on, yet too much pressure will certainly break the line, and you will lose the fish. You are in a much better situation if you have walked the fish toward shore, into shallow water. That way your rod tip is not way up in the air, bent in a dangerous curve, with the line threatening to break. Walking the fish in, rod down, keeps the pressure on, but not so much that the line is in danger of breaking off. When you walk a fish in, control stays with the angler, not the fish.


RELEASING THE FISH

If you are going to release the fish, handle it as little as possible. Handle it with care. Get a secure hold on the tail, a hold which causes no harm at all to the fish. Squeezing a fish too tightly can damage internal organs. Each time you touch a fish, it loses important protective scales and slime. The proper hold is to grip the tail and perhaps support the fish's belly, if you can. Try, if possible, to keep it out of the rocks, where, it may thrash about and might injure itself.

As you get ready to release it, make sure the fish's head is facing deep water, away from the bank, toward the current, so that water can move through its gills, helping it to recover. Hold the fish upright in this position for several moments, letting it relax, recuperate. It will move when it is ready and when it does, its chances of survival are much better than if you had simply removed the hook and let the fish sink back into the shallow water at the edge of the shore. Once the fish has moved off, continue to watch it for as long as you can to make sure it has fully recovered. If it begins to flounder again, try to reach it and lift. Repeat the same steps, holding it, head into the current, letting it rest and recover.

The question of release is a little tricky when it comes to salmon. After all, they are in the river to spawn and after they spawn, they will die. Even so, most salmon fishermen will keep only what they intend to eat and release the rest, so that they may live out their remaining lives naturally.

With steelhead, it's different. Many do not die after spawning. They are a beautiful, wild fish with a limited range and population. Take what legal hatchery-bred fish you intend to eat and release the wild ones.

As for me, I let all steelhead go because I want them to be there the next time I fish them. I always want there to be wild, beautiful runs of steelhead.

There are only a few other moments in fly fishing for big gamefish, that can match the thrill and joy of fishing, taking, and releasing big steelhead and salmon. There is no greater angling challenge, as far as I am concerned, and few angling experiences that are as satisfying or as memorable.


## FISHING FROM A BOAT

Though my personal preference is to fish from the shore, sometimes when you're fly fishing for Pacific salmon, it's nice to have a boat handy so you can chase fish if necessary.

Boat or pram fishing for Pacific salmon is immensely popular in northern California and southern Oregon. In fact, I think that this method originated in that area. Over time, it has proven to be a very effective method for catching the big chrome-bright ocean-run fish just as they are coming into the mouths of freshwater rivers for their spawn.

Boat fishing has many applications. Occasionally you'll encounter a situation where the salmon will be holding out in big, deep water that is simply unreachable from the shoreline. Or perhaps the stream bottom drops off sharply, prohibiting you from wading out far enough for an effective cast.

Or, sometimes Pacific salmon school-up in the lower waters of a river. This happens, for example, if the water is really low or there hasn't been a lot of rain or big tides. These fish will circle and hold in that lower water. And sometimes, if the terrain doesn't allow it, you'll have to use a boat to fish it. It's a great situation because you can actually pound those fish and get a lot of action. They are eager and great biters, though you do have to approach them delicately as they can really spook and move farther downriver. When I encounter this situation, it is oftentimes in slow water. In that case, I might use a little bit longer leader, say as long as 5, 6, or 7 feet (though a 7-foot leader would be rare). In these type situations, a boat may allow you to maneuver yourself into a good fishing position that would otherwise be unavailable to you.

An added advantage of fishing from a boat is that oftentimes you can get a nice long swing of the fly line and fly at the end of the drift. Salmon will frequently follow your fly and actually hit it at the very end of the drift, or just as you begin your line pick-up for the next cast.

The downside of fishing from a boat is that it can be awkward and difficult. You are always worried about rocking the boat or falling out or stepping on your line or hitting someone or getting something caught in your line when you're casting. I also think fishing from a boat is much more tiring physically. On shore, you can stretch and move around a little bit more — it is not as confining. And fishing from a boat restricts how much water you can cover. Fishing from shore allows you to cover the water more effectively most of the time, and also gives you greater control over the presentation.

But there are no hard fast rules, you can consistently and effectively catch salmon both from a boat and from shore. I don't think that there is only one way to catch salmon because I've taken them in many, many situations.

One of my favorite ways to fish for Pacific salmon is in tidal areas. In tidal areas, especially on high tides, salmon will push into the mouth of rivers, but they won't necessarily blow right through the area right away. Many times they'll hesitate, hold up, or travel slowly in the tidal water.

If you know their traveling waters and the lanes in which they're moving (often this can be identified simply by looking out and seeing them roll or jump or surface as they are moving up into freshwater), then you have a superb opportunity of hooking a lot of fish coming through. Simply cast out, allowing your line to sink and swing, secure in the knowledge that you're making consistently good presentations in the right area of the river that is loaded with fish.

OVERLEAF: *Donna and Jim Teeny with a sockeye salmon on the Kanektok River, Alaska.*

CHAPTER FOUR

# TACKLE FOR STEELHEAD AND SALMON

## STEELHEAD TACKLE

### RODS

When it comes to steelhead rods, for me the sensible choice would be a 9 to a 10-foot rod — nothing less in size. My favorite steelhead size is a 10-foot rod with an 8-weight line. I like the extra length because of the additional control and power it provides. With a rod this long, I believe you have better lifting power and control of the line. It also enables you to roll cast, mend, and pick up line easier.

There is as much variety among steelhead fly rods as there is with trout rods. Despite all the new rod technologies, for example, there are many steelhead anglers who still refuse to fish with anything but bamboo. Others prefer boron. My experience and personal preference keeps me with graphite. I like graphite because it is a material full of power and yet capable of a great deal of finesse. I like its faster action, the fact that though it is incredibly light, its power and muscle never detract from its amazing responsiveness and sensitivity.

Another reason for going with graphite is that most graphite rods on the market today feature a very strong butt section, which is important in steelhead fishing. The strong butt section balances out the graphite's fast tip action. And the butt section really helps in firmly setting the hook on bigger fish. Yet the tip is supple enough to relay the lightest strike. With graphite, you can really feel the fish throughout the line and the rod.

I have never used the two-handed rods which have become so popular. I love to kid around with the guys that use them, I've said, "Gee, they are so big, you could also use them as a wading staff!" Two-handed rods are quite heavy and I think using them is a lot of work. You are throwing a lot more weight, a lot more rod around. It takes significantly more effort to get that fly out there. Also, I tend to fish smaller rivers and have really never felt the need to use anything longer than a 10-foot rod.

The guys who use two-handed rods truly enjoy them. I've had people tell me that the line control is unbelievable, I'm sure that's true. The one absolute advantage that the two-handed rod has over the single-handed rod is that it can deliver great distances on the casts. If a person wants to work at it and cast at a distance of over 100 feet, there is no question that he should be using a two-handed rod. For example, on the Thompson River or the main watershed of the Skeena in British Columbia, the Deschutes in Oregon, or the Cowlitz or Skagit in Washington — rivers where you want to get a big, long cast across the entire stream — a two-handed rod can be a real asset if you've loaded your rig properly; whereas most anglers cannot consistently obtain such great distances with single-handed rods.

## REELS

When going for steelhead, I like to use a single-action reel with a large diameter and an adjustable drag which gives me excellent line control and permits me to pick up line quickly.

I set the adjustable drag so that no matter how hard and fast the line is being pulled off by the fish, there will be no ruinous backlash, lock-up, or break off. I always make sure my drag is adjusted before I get on the water and start fishing. If your drag is not tightened down enough, a big fish that takes a lot of line out rapidly will almost certainly foul or jam the reel, with the line overrunning the spool, creating a bird's nest of backlash. In such situations, once the reel jams up so that you are unable to feed the fish additional line, its next run will likely break your backing/line/leader rigging at its most vulnerable point.

Palming the reel is something I am always doing, as well. Consequently, I like a reel with a definite outside rim so that I can palm it and put additional drag pressure on the line and have good line control. But note that you have to be careful not to over-palm the reel. Many fly fishermen prefer a reel with anti-reverse for just this reason. Anti-reverse reels are certainly nice and very sophisticated, but I just haven't gotten into the habit of using them.

Once you learn when and how to keep your fingers clear of the reel and line, palming, for me, is less complicated. If you hook a really big steelhead, after you have immediately cleared the line, you should fight the fish using not only your rod, but your reel as well. Never try to strip in line on a big fish by hand; go to the reel. Trying to work a fish off the line will cause only headaches and trouble, since your line will get twisted in all directions, likely resulting in a lost fish.

It is just smart angling, I think, especially when fishing for steelhead and salmon, to load the spools for whatever reels you're going to be using pretty close to full. I think this is advantageous because with a fully packed spool you are picking up line with every turn of the reel, whereas with less than a fully packed spool you have to expend a lot of time and wasted turns before you actually start picking up line. Also,

I've found that with a packed spool, slack is much easier to control, and line pick-up is quicker and smoother.

### BACKING

When fishing for running steelhead, I strongly recommend fishing with nothing less than 75 yards of backing. And 100 or 200 yards is even better, particularly if you are fishing on big water. I personally prefer braided-Dacron backing. It is sturdy, long-lived, and is a good choice of backing for any fish where consistent knot strength is important. I like my backing to have color. Many backings being sold today are either beige or white, and I find them hard to see, especially in low-light conditions. But with colored or high visibility backing, I can see when a fish is running, what is happening, what line the fish has, what line I've got left on my reel. My favorite choice is bright orange braided-Dacron backing.

I believe that for big fish, you should use backing of no less than 30-pound test. I do not think it is smart fishing to have your backing weaker than your fly line. Because once a fish is into the backing, that backing needs to be strong enough to hold it, to stay with the fish. When you are going after big fish, you need strong line and equally strong backing.

Of course, if you are stream fishing for smaller fish, casting lines as light as, say, 2, 3, 4 or 5-weight, then you can go down to backing as light as 10 or 12-pound test. So select your backing by the average size of the species of fish you are angling for: big fish, 30-pound backing, at least; smaller fish, yet still large, 20-pound test; and smaller fish, at least 12-pound test.

### LINES

The floating line is ubiquitous among fly fishermen, as common as the beat-up fishing hat or overstuffed fly-fishing vest. The floating line is versatile, easy to cast, easy to see, and easy to mend. It is the line most fly fishermen began their fly fishing with, and what most people use all the time. But, for me, the floating line is hardly the most sophisticated of fly lines. In my opinion, the more skilled and advanced a fly fisherman becomes, the less he should rely so heavily on the floating line. In steelhead and salmon fishing at least, the floating line should, at best, be thought of as a part-time line. There are just too many situations you encounter with these fish in which a floating line simply won't work; situations in which only a sinking-tip or a full-sinking line will do.

Keep in mind that where the fish is holding in the water column is dependent on a number of factors — the water temperature and condition, fishing pressure, and so on. If the water is perfect, clear, with a temperature between 40 and 50 degrees Fahrenheit, and the steelhead is not at all spooky, you may be able to work successfully into a spot with a floating line. But more times than not that fish is not at the surface. (It's simply not a natural act for migratory fish to take food at the surface, though resident trout will certainly do so.) You need to start and stick with a sink-tip or a full-sinking line, something that will get your fly down at least five feet deep in the water column. If nothing happens at that water depth, you may want to go a little deeper perhaps even down to 10 feet (if the water level of the river is high, for example) or go to a sinking shooting-taper — whatever is necessary to get the fly down to where the fish is, whether it is two feet or 15 feet.

Today most line manufacturers offer a 10-foot sinking-tip line, though some offer longer sinking-tips, especially on shooting-tapers. Properly used, sinking-tip and full-sinking lines are among the most versatile of fly-fishing lines. Such lines, which have been designed and calibrated to very accurate sink rates, can be deadly against steelhead, particularly in deeper pools, riffles, and tail-outs. The idea is to cast far enough upstream of fish holding deep so that the line and fly will have enough time to sink to the right depth in the water column, then swing naturally by the fish. I much prefer to use a sinking line rather than a weighted fly, because I do not believe weighted flies come close to matching the look or behavior of a natural food.

There are as many different line tapers as there are lines — weight-forward tapers, rocket tapers, double tapers, triangle tapers, tapers designed for specific species of fish (bass, bonefish, tarpon, steelhead, etc.) numerous types of shooting-tapers, even lines with no taper (the level line). It gets confusing. But for steelhead — indeed for a great deal of trout water and trout fishing situations — the weight-forward taper seems the most versatile.

Shooting-tapers attached to level lines work well, as do my T-Series lines (which I'll be discussing below).

Another good alternative to the weight-forward taper for many anglers is the double-taper line, which has a heavy mid-section tapering down on both ends of the line. Of course, when you fish a double-taper line, you are actually fishing only one tapered end. It has the economic advantage that when you wear out one tapered end of line, you can reverse the line on your reel and then switch to the unused taper on the other end. It's like fishing with a new line. Also, many anglers believe that double-tapered lines provide greater presentation accuracy when used on big rods in the very heavy line weights.

Regarding weight, for bigger steelhead, you really need to use 8 and 9-weight lines, I think. Though lighter lines can work well on steelhead, not just the 8-weight, but even lighter still, in certain water conditions. If you are spotting fish that are on the small side, you can even fish steelhead with a 6-weight line without sacrificing any advantages at all.

## TEENY LINES

Now, I don't want to give you the impression that I am the only capable person manufacturing quality sinking lines for steelhead and salmon. There are certainly many other manufacturers making good sinking lines: Scientific Anglers/3M and Cortland, for example, just to name two of the more prominent manufacturers.

But I would like to tell you a little bit about my T-Series of lines, because despite my self-interest in your using one, they really are deadly on fish such as steelhead and salmon, which typically hold deep in the water column.

You see, I developed the T-Series of lines partly because the behavior of steelhead is so unlike that of any other trout, requiring that they be fished with a different technique. When you are fishing for steelhead, delicacy is really not as important a consideration as you might think. You can be klutzy and get out there and catch fish, because usually with steelhead, you are not casting your fly directly to the fish. Rather, you are casting your fly line and fly above the fish, allowing it to sink and then swim or drift down to it.

I developed the Teeny lines really out of personal necessity. For years, I bought shooting-tapers that were 30 feet long and spliced them to a running line that consisted of a level floating line. But when I finished tying the connection between the shooting-taper and running line, I never knew whether or not I had produced a good knot or a good splice. I was always bothered by the protruding knot, and it frequently caught on one of my rod guides, causing a break-off and a lost fish. Or when casting, I found that if I pulled some of the shooting-taper into the rod tip and guides, when I would make my next cast and shoot out line, the connection knot would sometimes snarl or catch in a guide or the tip, resulting in a poor cast. This problem also placed an additional technique burden on me, in that in addition to concentrating on the really important task at hand, that is, watching and tracking the fish and my fly, I had to make sure that I never pulled the knot connection inside my rod tip.

Also, a 30-foot-long shooting-taper was a lot for me to handle, because the rivers in Oregon and in Washington — the places where I fish most frequently — generally do not provide enough space for a long back cast. In such areas, with only a limited amount of space for the back cast, you are much better off with a shorter shooting-taper that requires less space on the back cast so that your fly will not hang up in the brush behind you.

First, I trimmed three feet off the tapers on both ends of the standard 30-foot shooting-taper, making it into a 24-foot-long shooting-taper. I then connected a running line to the shooting-taper. Believe me, it made a world of difference. The shorter head sank evenly and made a better presentation.

The remaining drawback to this first adaptation, however, was still that lousy connection knot that continued to hang up or snarl on one of my rod guides. I was determined to figure out a way to eliminate the connection knot altogether, to make a sinking head with a running line with which any fly fisherman could cast and fight fish with relative ease and without having to worry about line snarls. I approached Scientific Anglers/3M, asking them if they would manufacture lines for me based on my specifications — colors, tapers, whatever. They agreed to do it, and thus was created the T-Series Teeny Nymph Lines.

Most of the lines in the T-Series (the 130-grain T-130, the 200-grain T-200, the 300-grain T-300, and the 400-grain T-400) consist of 24 feet of Deep Water Express line combined in a one-piece, smooth knotless connection with 58 feet of level floating line — creating a line with an overall length of 82 feet and with the smooth configuration of a conventional fly line. The single exception is the 500-grain T-500 line, which has a sinking section of 28 feet of Deep Water Express combined with a floating section or 54 feet, yielding a line with an overall length of 82 feet.

(I later began manufacturing a saltwater series of longer lines, because a number of saltwater anglers — who are generally not bothered by lack of space for a long back cast — complained to me that on their long casts they could routinely carry outside their rod tip the entire 24-foot sinking section as well as a number of feet of lighter running line which would sag down below the rod tip and adversely affect their casts. For this series of saltwater lines, therefore we lengthened the overall line to 100 feet, consisting of 30 feet of Deep Water Express line combined with 70 feet of level floating line.)

Using the T-Series is very easy; the chart below indicates what rod sizes each line can be used with. Or, if you prefer, since the lines do not have a taper in the sinking section, you can cut off a few feet of this section to customize the line for your own rod and casting style.

| T-Series Lines | Rod Size |
| --- | --- |
| T-130 | 4, 5, 6 |
| T-200 | 5, 6, 7, 8 |
| T-300 | 8, 9, 10 |
| T-400 and T-500 | 9 or higher |

| Teeny Saltwater Lines | Rod Size |
| --- | --- |
| TS-250 | 6, 7, 8, 9 |
| TS-350 | 8, 9, 10, 11 |
| TS-450 | 9, 10, 11, 12 |
| TS-550 | 9, 10, 11, 12, 13 |
| TS-650 | 10, 11, 12, 13, 14 |
| TS-750 | 11, 12, 13, 14, 15 |

These lines are perfectly balanced and have a uniform-sink rate which contributes greatly to line control and consistent casting. And, since there's no taper in the sinking portion of the lines, they will sink uniformly throughout their entire length. This differs from regular tapered sinking lines in that oftentimes with those type lines you can get what I call "tip lag." That is, after you make your cast and the line swing begins, the high density mid-section of the shooting-taper of the line is sinking down deep where the fish are, but the front tapered portion (where your fly is) is riding higher in the water. So, your fly is going to be several feet higher in the water column than the rest of your line — way above the fish!

Recognizing this problem, most of the leading line manufacturers now produce a uniform-sinking line.

The T-series are not lead-core lines. Instead, tiny particles of tungsten (which is an environmentally safe product) are embedded right into the coating of the lines. So, they actually feel like conventional fly lines. The difference being that when coiled, the lead-core lines stay coiled. On the other hand, the T-Series lines have excellent memory and will tend to return to a straight configuration.

An added feature of these lines is that they are all color-coded. All the sinking sections of the lines are manufactured in a dark color (dark brown in the T-Series, dark green in the Saltwater Series) to prevent them from spooking fish. Such a darkly colored sinking section combined with a brightly colored level floating line, which the fish won't see, but which the angler can, is a great advantage. For example, because the floating sections are brightly colored, an angler can tell instantly when the sinking section is within a foot or two of the rod tip. And, this color coding of the line not only indicates to the angler exactly where the true balance of the line is; it also provides a clear indication of how much line remains underwater, so the angler can gauge exactly when to pick it up

*T-Series and Teeny Saltwater Fly Lines* — from top to bottom: *T-130, T-200, T-300, T-400, T-500, Teeny Mini-Tip, TS-250, TS-350, TS-450, TS-650.* ➤

for the next cast. I believe this gives the angler better line control than a uniform-sinking line, which is colored identically throughout its entire length. What this does for the average angler, I think, is that it helps take away some of the guesswork about when he should pick up his line. And that actually helps most people cast a greater distance with less effort.

I developed another specialized line, the Mini-Tip line, a bit later. I like to fish lakes from the shoreline, and oftentimes, the weedy areas around the shore are difficult to make good presentations into with a standard sink-tip line. While a 10-foot sink tip line gets your fly into the weeds quickly and sinks it deeply, I've found that often fish are not feeding in the deep water but in the shallower water closer to shore.

I wanted a sinking-tip line that was shorter, a line to which I could add a long leader and cast out above fish and slowly drift the fly to them. The Mini-Tip fits the bill. It is a weight-forward floating line combined in a smooth knotless connection to 5 feet of Hi-Speed Hi-D sinking line.

The Mini-Tip line is also effective on streams, for example in Alaska, where you will encounter sockeye and chum salmon suspended at just under the surface or at the mid-level of the water column. In fact, sometimes steelhead will also suspend just below the surface or at mid-levels of the water column — particularly spring/summer-run fish. Since such fish are not suspended on the bottom, you don't want to get down too deep. A Mini-Tip line with a long leader puts that fly just under the surface but not down on the bottom. In steelhead fishing, I usually use a 9 to 12-foot leader with this line. In Alaska, I'll shorten the leader from 6 to 8 feet.

I've caught everything from trout to halibut on these T-Series lines. For steelhead and salmon, I've learned that the T-200, T-300, T-400, and T-500 are best. These lines get the fly down to the fish, wherever it is in the water column, and they do it accurately.

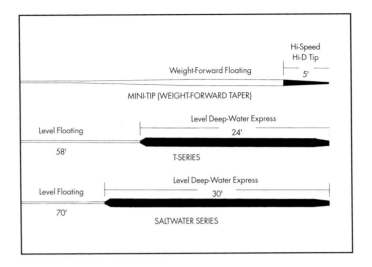

Hi-Speed
Hi-D Tip

Weight-Forward Floating | 5'

MINI-TIP (WEIGHT-FORWARD TAPER)

Level Deep-Water Express

Level Floating

24'

58'

T-SERIES

Level Deep-Water Express

Level Floating

30'

70'

SALTWATER SERIES

*Teeny Line Configurations*

Remember that in a lot of fishing situations you're going to have to use your own judgment as to what line you're going to select. Reading the water — the water speed and water depth particularly — is critical with the T-Series lines as well as with the sinking lines of other manufacturers. For example, when I'm using my lines, I'll walk up to heavy, deep water and say, "Well, that's T-400 water." Or I may walk up to a piece of shallow water, where the current speed is a little slower and say, "This is T-200 water." And so on. Once you get into the habit of doing this, you can place your line down to any depth in the water column that you want, on any type of water, and present the fly just exactly where you think the fish are holding. This will give you a big advantage over other fishermen; this is going to make you a better fisherman and is going to ultimately help you to hook and catch more fish.

Whatever lines you choose to purchase, I highly recommend that you carry a wide variety of lines with you, anywhere you go. My personal preference is to carry a weight-forward floating line, a Mini-Tip line, and the entire selection of grain weights of the T-Series. That's a lot of lines; probably more than the average fly fisherman ever carries to a stream. But for the variety of stream conditions and fish-holding positions that you encounter fly fishing to steelhead and salmon, such a large selection will give you the definite advantage of being flexible enough to adapt to whatever situation may occur. Whether the fish are on the surface, just below it, at mid-level, or at any variety of bottom depths, my fly is going to be there with them! Yours should be, too, if you want to catch fish!

### Leaders And Tippets

Steelhead are wary, extremely cautious fish. So clear leaders and tippets are essential. Using clear tippet monofilament gives the illusion — so important in successful steelhead fishing — of the fly being out on the water by itself, unconnected, just as though it were a real insect floating freely on the surface of the water or under it. But with time, all monofilament begins to lose its strength, wears out, and eventually breaks down. Given this fact, it is important that you check your leader and tippet material often and that you change it as soon as it begins to get too soft.

Selecting leaders and tippets depends largely on the immediate fishing situation you are facing. If I know, for example, that I am going to be doing some lake fishing, I usually go with long leaders, from 9 to 12 feet. Using a longer leader helps assure me that the fish will, hopefully, not see my fly line at all, but will see only the fly, which is all I want them to see.

If you are fishing deep pools, you also are going to have to go to a long leader, at least a 9 to 12-foot leader of clear monofilament with about an 8-pound-test tippet. And really

*Anglers fishing for steelhead on the Three Rivers, Oregon.* ➤

pay attention to your cast, making it as accurate as possible. In such deep pool situations, where the fish are suspending in clear water, that fly has got to look natural, and the shadow of the fly line can't be thrown over the fish. So, a long leader is absolutely necessary. Then it's just the waiting: the concentration, keeping your finger tip delicately on the line, feeling for that slight wrinkle, that almost imperceptible twitch that is the strike, and waiting that one instant before setting the hook — because often if you do not wait that one extra second, you will yank the fly from the fish's still open mouth.

Let me re-emphasize that you need to continually experiment with leader lengths. In dirty or moving-water situations — riffles, moving current, broken water, for example — long leaders are not really that important. In fact, years ago, Lefty advised me to cut down on my leader length for presentations in this type water. At the time, I thought he was crazy, how can you not spook a fish with a short leader? But I took his advice, and found that in moving-water situations short leaders really do work. I usually use 3 or 4-foot leaders, and go down to even a 2-foot leader if the water is high and murky. On coho salmon in a tail-out on the Kalama one year I even used a leader as short as 8 inches, which was just a piece of monofilament tied from the end of my fly line to the fly. These fish were in a very deep slot and I had to keep shortening my leader until I finally got the fly down to the right depth. I nailed four or five fish, one after the other.

If you find that with a short leader the fish are spooking, then go to a longer or lighter leader. Again, you need to experiment. The more things you try, the better angler you're going to be, and the more fish you're going to hook.

You have to know what your leader can and cannot do, as well. Will a 10-foot leader, for instance, work well with a sinking line? No, because while your line would be sinking, your long and lighter leader (and fly) would be rising in the water.

On rivers where the water is running low and the trout are holding in the deeper pools, again, I think longer leaders are the wisest choice. Shorter leaders, particularly when fishing for steelhead and salmon in low water, put the fly line on the water much too close to the fish, usually spooking them. Again, a longer leader and tippet will keep the fly line and its shadow away from the fish and a good presentation will leave them with only the fly to consider.

I recommend you begin experimenting on leader length by starting out with at least 9 feet. Go up or down from that length until you are satisfied that you have enough length to get your fly where you want it in reference to the fish without showing the line, or without throwing a shadow on the water.

Remember, the whole key to this type of fishing is to keep your fly down deep as long as you can, at the proper level. And the more natural your presentation of the fly is, the more fish you are going to hook consistently.

The knot of choice for me in joining leader and tippet is the tried-and-true blood knot; and the leader material I use has to be able to give me a knot strength as close to 100 percent as possible. Moistening the line before drawing a blood knot together is a good habit to get into. The moisture reduces the friction on the line and assures a much better knot. A little moisture applied to almost any knot before it is tied down will only improve its performance.

## SALMON TACKLE

The tackle needed to fish for salmon is, again, similar to steelhead tackle. No matter what kind of rig you put together, make sure everything — rod, reel, line, tippet, etc. — is properly balanced weight-wise and size-wise. Then your casting will be so much easier as will be your presentation of the fly.

## Rods And Reels

For chinook, chum, and coho salmon, I prefer a long graphite rod — between 9 and 10 feet — loaded with an 8 or 9-weight line. Most of the big graphite rods being manufactured today by the leading rod makers are excellent, and really handle the heavier lines well in every possible angling situation — from line mending as well as any number of casts such as roll casts or any of the long, difficult, precise casts.

For sockeye salmon I will either stay with a 9 or 10-foot rod with an 8-weight line. A 9-foot rod is perfect for pink salmon, although for the pinks I reduce my line weight to a 6.

With salmon, as with steelhead, I stay with my single-action reel, one that balances with whatever rod I am using, one with a definite outside rim for easy palming. With salmon, as with steelhead, adjustable drag is mandatory. Always pre-set the drag for the fishing conditions you expect to encounter.

## Backing

Put on at least 100 yards of strong backing. With chinook, coho, and chum salmon, the backing ought to be at least 30-pound test. Although you can get by with using lighter backing and less of it when fishing for pinks, I still recommend the heavier backing and lots of it. With salmon runs, you are never sure what you might hook into. If you're fishing Alaska and are after pinks, odds are pretty good that you may hook sockeye and chinook, too. And if that happens when you're using the lighter backing, chances are you'll end up losing the fly line, and more importantly, the big salmon. If you're after the lighter end with the pinks, then 50 to 100 yards of backing is okay in 20-pound test.

My preference for backing, as with steelhead fishing, is braided-Dacron line, which is extremely durable and maintains its strength much longer than regular monofilament. Monofilament expands and contracts with varying weather conditions which sometimes can actually warp a spool or reel. Also, monofilament deteriorates quickly. I've stored away 20-pound mono for the year, and re-tested it at the beginning of the next fishing season, only to find that it tested at only 12 or 15 pounds.

## LINES

For your choice of fly lines, you have to think about what type of fish you're going after and what the fishing conditions will be. To cover all the possible situations for salmon, take along a floating line, a sinking-tip line, and a full-sinking line. Your casting rig with at least these three type lines should cover just about any situation you will encounter with salmon. One will work, no matter the weather, water conditions, or mood of the fish.

Remember, as conditions change, never be afraid to change your rig accordingly, be it a change of line and leader, or of tippet and fly. Fish do not have to adapt; fly fishermen do. If the salmon are acting spooky, go with a longer leader, something that will leave the fish with nothing but the fly to consider. If the water is discolored and you are fishing in close to riffles or pocket water, then go to a shorter tippet or maybe change flies.

With salmon, bigger flies (#2s and #4s) seem to work better than the smaller sizes. The exception may be when you are fishing them in clearer, calmer water, say, in shallow pools. Then presentation becomes critical and you might want to try some smaller flies, though I do not fish for salmon with a fly smaller than a #8 or #10.

OVERLEAF: *John Dusa with a wild buck steelhead on the Kispiox River in British Columbia.*

## CHAPTER FIVE

# STEELHEAD AND SALMON FLIES

During the typical run of steelhead and salmon, you have the opportunity to use almost any fly you want — wet flies, nymphs, streamers, even the occasional dry fly. However, I have found that the most effective fly against running steelhead and salmon is the nymph. Leech imitations can also be effective, as can flash flies — little deadly attractor flies tied with Crystal Flash — which the fish simply can't stay away from.

No matter where you are fishing, it is always a good idea to check with local anglers and at local fly shops to see what sizes and patterns are working at the time you are going to fish. But there is no firm, fast rule on fly pattern and size. Never be scared to experiment, throw something different. It just might be the fly to get the fish stirred up.

Fly selection is always something of a perplexing subject with me because I have been fishing exclusively with Teeny Nymphs, Teeny Leeches, and Teeny Flash Flies since 1971. These work extremely well for me. Indeed, I've yet to find a fish or a fishing situation where they do not work, so I stick with them. Still, I know that there is an incredible variety of steelhead and salmon patterns, many with proven reputations.

In working with the Teeny flies, I can tell you what I've discovered about flies — that color can be an extremely important factor, with the darker colors tending to get the best results. But there are times when the colors of ginger, or even pink or purple, can be deadly. Situation and fish behavior determine the proper fly. You have to experiment, find out what is working at that moment on the water as you fish.

The same rule applies to fly size. When fishing for steelhead and salmon, I tend to start off using flies in the larger sizes. If these appear to be scaring the fish off, or are not tempting them in the least, then I will start dropping down in size, though usually I will not use anything smaller than a #10 for steelhead and salmon. Indeed, normally for steelhead and salmon, I'll consistently use sizes #2 and #4, and will only drop down to #6s, #8s, and #10s for really spooky fish.

In regard to hooks, stay with hard steel and keep them sharp, because the strike of steelhead and salmon is so often gentle. They don't strike a fly so much as pick it up; so it is extremely easy to lose a fish to a missed strike on a dull hook.

## TEENY FLY PATTERNS

As I've said, my fly boxes are always full of — what else — Teeny Nymphs, Leeches, and our Flash Fly patterns. I began designing the Teeny Nymphs back in 1962 and have been using them ever since, testing them against as many species of gamefish as possible in as many different angling situations as possible.

I now fish my own patterns exclusively. In addition to their being extremely successful for me, I figured when I started my business that if I was going to put my name on the patterns, then I should fish them.

### Teeny Nymphs

Like my fly lines, the Teeny Nymph was developed out of necessity, with some luck involved. In May 1962, my friend,

Dan Schacher, and I were going to go to East Lake in central Oregon, a place we fished a lot. The trout in East Lake were the size of steelhead or small salmon, but on our last trip or two we had had little success in fishing for them. Therefore, the night before our next trip, I decided to tie up a new pattern. My dad had suggested making it as ugly as possible. So, I picked out the ugliest material I could find, which was a ringed-neck pheasant tail feather. I put a #8 hook in the vise, stripped off some feathers from the tail, wrapped them around the hook, and created a #8 Teeny Nymph, not knowing at that time what it was.

I had no idea whether or not this pattern was going to work. But from my first cast on the next day, it was a killer. Because it was so deadly, we originally gave it a strange and exotic name — the "Abduli" — because we didn't want other fishermen to find out about it. When anglers came up and asked about the fly, we told them it was an Abduli. Naturally, they could never find one in any fly shop, so we were able to keep it a secret for about nine years until I started my company.

The fly was originally tied in a natural color. I didn't try it out in other colors until we started the business in 1971, and, at the suggestion of other anglers, we experimented with different colors. For example, trying an antique gold color to imitate a stonefly or an insect green for a damselfly, etc.

When I originally designed this pattern, as I said, it was for big East Lake trout that we could see cruising along. At that point I was 16 years old and hadn't done any fly fishing for steelhead or salmon. I had never even considered using this new pattern on steelhead or salmon, because I had been taught that steelhead needed attractor colors and salmon needed brighter colors, and that both species needed flash and something to entice them to bite.

Teeny Nymphs and Leeches hold (or have held at one time) 20 IGFA World Records over the years, and I think that clearly the Teeny Nymph has proven itself as a good, reliable fly, one that ought to be in every angler's fly box.

The reason I believe that the Teeny Nymph has been so deadly is that it is a suggestive fly pattern; it is not a duplicate of any particular insect or hatch. It looks like a lot of different things. In the darker, more natural colors, it really has excellent fish appeal because it looks like something tasty to eat. In addition, the fly offers a good silhouette; the fibers have a lot of natural colors and natural iridescence, looking like caddis, hellgrammittes, periwinkles, and lots of different things that fish have in their normal diet.

I tie it in several sizes — the smallest being #14. Although before I actually started marketing the fly, I did tie them down to size #20, and I did catch some trout on those smaller sizes. But now my fly tyers refuse to tie anything smaller than a #14. And anglers have found that in Oregon, at least, we really don't need to go much smaller than a #10.

After starting off with that original #8 fly, I later tried tying the fly on a #4 hook, which made it a double body. I figured that this might possibly look like two insects mating, and that the fish would think that they are getting more of a mouthful. The #4 has ended up being my and my wife's Donna single favorite fly for everything from bluegill to salmon — it's just a killer.

Years of fishing the rivers of the Pacific Northwest have taught me that the Teeny Nymph is especially good when used on nervous steelhead and edgy salmon. If the fish are under any kind of pressure or if they are being a little bit selective, they definitely will take the Teeny Nymph more often. I think this is because the patterns are smaller, don't have a tail, and

*Teeny Nymphs* — from left to right, top row: *Natural, Hot Green*; 2nd row: *Ginger, Flame Orange*; 3rd row: *Black, Antique Gold*; 4th row: *Purple*; 5th row: *Insect Green.* ➤

their body profile is smaller. And they don't seem to spook the fish the way bigger, gaudier flies do.

Brightly colored flies frequently scare off steelhead and salmon. For most situations, I tend to go with something dark, and I will stick with the dark-colored pattern as long as the fish are holding, even if, at first, they may show little or no interest. Since with steelhead and salmon, in most situations, presentation is as important as the fly you are using, a good presentation, along with a dark nymph, will usually spark some interest.

And by dark, I mean really dark. The old angling saying about "I don't care what color it is as long as it's black" holds a lot of truth. In fly fishing for steelhead and salmon, black is basic; it casts a great shadow, can be used in clear or off-color water, and more often than not will out produce any other color or combination of colors.

Among my flies, the only dressing that comes close to the performance of the darkly colored nymphs is a dark insect green. But even it is speckled with black.

Last May we went to Russia and did extremely well on the Russian rainbows in the natural, antique gold, and ginger colors, as well as black. These were big, wild rainbow trout that had never seen a fly and those were the colors they definitely preferred.

If you closely examine the Teeny Nymphs, you'll see they combine several colors. For example, the natural pattern actually consists of three different colors — an iridescent green, a brown, and a black. I believe that combining several colors into a fly pattern assists in making it look buggy.

Also, I think the key to creating or designing a good fly pattern is to make it look natural and appealing — but not necessarily attractive. Over the years, we have found that the prettiest flies, the flashiest ones, don't necessarily catch the most or the biggest fish.

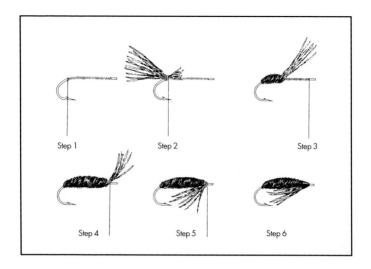

Step 1    Step 2    Step 3

Step 4    Step 5    Step 6

*Tying a Teeny Nymph*

*Tying Instructions for the Teeny Nymph* — If you like to tie your own flies, tying the Teeny Nymph is relatively easy. The amount of pheasant feathers that you use for the pattern depends upon how bulky or how sparse a fly you want and, of course, upon the hook size. It's completely up to the individual tyer. For a typical #6 pattern, proceed as follows:

*Step 1*) Wrap the hook with thread starting from the eye as shown in the illustration above.

*Step 2*) Add approximately a 1/2-inch of ringed-neck pheasant tail feathers and wrap thread to the eye.

*Step 3*) Wrap the feathers tightly, clockwise around the hook.

*Step 4*) Secure feathers at the eye.

*Step 5*) Pull the remainder of the feathers under the eye, pointing back, securing them with thread.

*Step 6*) Wrap the thread back and forth to shape the head. Secure and cut the thread.

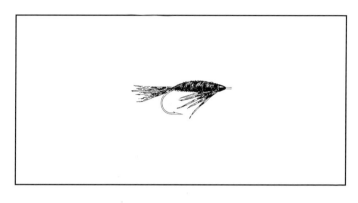

*The Teeny Leech*

### TEENY LEECHES

I developed my second favorite pattern, the Teeny Leech, about eight or nine years ago. You'll note that it's simply a variation of the Teeny Nymph in that this pattern just has a tail. Sizes of the pattern range from #2 to #12 and, like the Teeny Nymph, the leeches come in a variety of nine colors — black, hot green, purple, ginger, flame orange, hot pink, antique gold, natural, and insect green.

I have found that this leech pattern offers a little bit bigger profile than the nymph, which really begins to put it more in the category of an attractor pattern. Of course, in clear water it doesn't really make a big difference, but in big or murky water, these leech patterns can be quite deadly.

*Tying Instructions for the Teeny Leech* — Follow the instructions for tying the Teeny Nymph (see page 135) *except* a butt section of feathers should be tied on between Steps 1 and 2 to create the tail.

*Teeny Leeches* — from left to right, top row: *Ginger, Hot Green*; 2nd row: *Natural, Hot Pink*; 3rd row: *Flame Orange, Insect Green*; 4th row: *Antique Gold, Black*. ➤

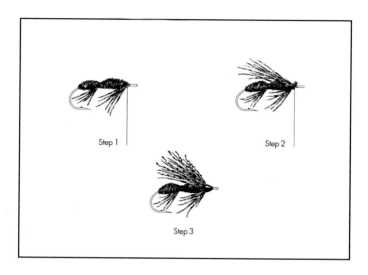

Step 1   Step 2

Step 3

*Tying a Teeny Flash Fly*

### TEENY FLASH FLIES

Our flash fly patterns came along a bit later. They are true attractor patterns in that about eight strands of Crystal Flash have been added to the basic two-tone color scheme. These patterns will work well on steelhead and salmon, tied in sizes #2 - #6. They are not, however, overall as consistently successful as the Teeny Nymph or Teeny Leech when tied in the darker colors.

The flash fly patterns tied in the bright colors do work well in Alaska and British Columbia. Also, in the fall, they are killer when going for salmon on the coasts of Oregon and Washington as well as in the Great Lakes area.

*Teeny Flash Flies* — from left to right, top row: *Orange/Ginger, Hot Green/Black*; 2nd row: *Ginger/Black, Hot Pink/Ginger*; 3rd row: *Purple/Black, Flame Orange/Black*. ➤

*Tying Instructions for the Teeny Flash Fly —*

*Step 1)* Follow the instructions for Steps 1 through 5 for making the Teeny Nymph (see page 135), except only wrap the feathers halfway up the shank and secure. Take another section of feathers and repeat from halfway point to eye.

*Step 2)* Before making the head, tie on another section of feathers as shown on page 138. Complete head.

*Step 3)* Add approximately 8 strands of Crystal Flash to the top hackle section.

## OTHER FAVORITE STEELHEAD
## AND SALMON FLY PATTERNS

If I were forced to use flies other than my own patterns for my steelhead and salmon fishing, the following 24 patterns would be my choice. I asked my good friend, Doug Stewart, to tie all the photographed models of these favorites for this book, including one of his own patterns. All of these patterns are wet flies, including a few riffle or waking patterns: the Greased Liner, Bucktail Coachman, and Juicy Bug. The only streamer is the Spruce Fly. There are no nymphs or leeches. The attractor patterns are: Del Cooper, Orange Comet, Babine Special, Polar Shrimp, Skykomish Sunrise, Umpqua Special, Brad's Brat, Thor, Golden Demon, and Fall Favorite. There are no dry flies.

While all of these patterns were designed primarily as steelhead flies, they will also work well on salmon. By species of salmon, here are my favorite selections:

*Steelhead and Salmon Patterns* — from left to right, top row: *Max Canyon, Tranquilizer*; 2nd row: *Purple Peril, Skunk*; 3rd row: *Green Butt Skunk, Del Cooper*; 4th row: *Dark Max, McLeod Ugly.* ➤

*Chinook salmon:* Babine Special, Polar Shrimp, Boss, Max Canyon.

*Coho salmon:* Babine Special, Polar Shrimp, Skykomish Sunrise, Orange Comet.

*Sockeye salmon:* All patterns.

*Chum salmon:* Green Butt Skunk, Dark Max, Brad's Brat, Thor.

*Pink salmon:* Max Canyon, Skunk, Umpqua Special, Fall Favorite.

By watershed, here are my favorite steelhead and salmon selections:

*Pacific Northwest, excluding British Columbia:* All patterns.

*British Columbia:* Purple Peril, Skykomish Sunrise, Babine Special, Brad's Brat, McLeod Ugly.

By water condition, here are my favorite steelhead and salmon selections:

*Low/clear water:* Max Canyon, Del Cooper, Golden Demon, Fall Favorite, Greased Liner.

*High/dirty water:* Dark Max, Stewart, McLeod Ugly, Boss.

Here are brief descriptions of the patterns:

1. *Max Canyon* — A Deschutes River pattern originated by Doug Stewart of Gresham, Oregon, this pattern is a combination of the colors from the Skunk and Brad's Brat (black and orange). Generally tied in sizes #2 - #6, this is an excellent all-purpose fly pattern for steelhead. Chinook salmon and pink salmon can be fished with it under a variety of conditions successfully. It is particularly effective in low, clear water. It is normally fished on a floating or sinking line with a wet-fly swing technique.

*Steelhead and Salmon Patterns* — from left to right, top row: *Juicy Bug, Bucktail Caddis*; 2nd row: *Spruce Fly, Bucktail Coachman*; 3rd row: *Stewart, Brad's Brat*; 4th row: *Golden Demon, Fall Favorite.* ➤

2. *Dark Max* — A variation of the Max Canyon, this pattern was originated by Larry Piatt of Prineville, Oregon. Tied in sizes #2 - #6, it works well in off-color water, especially on the Deschutes and Sandy rivers, to steelhead and chum salmon. It's best fished either on a wet-fly swing or dead drift.

3. *Stewart* — This pattern is another variation of the Max Canyon, originated by Marty Sherman of Portland, Oregon, and named after Doug Stewart. Generally tied in sizes #2 - #6, this is a versatile dark steelhead fly pattern, particularly effective in high, off-color water. It can be fished with a floating line with a wet-fly swing technique.

4. *Skunk* — This pattern first appeared on the North Umpqua in the 1940s. It is usually tied in sizes #4 and #6, and is highly effective on steelhead and pink salmon. Fished with a wet-fly swing on a floating or sinking line, this pattern is effective in all streams and in all sorts of conditions.

5. *Green Butt Skunk* — This fly is a variation of the Skunk as well as the Black Bear-Green Butt pattern, a popular Atlantic salmon fly. Its originator is unknown, but it is frequently used on the Deschutes River. It can be tied in sizes #4 and #6, and should be fished with a wet-fly swing, using a floating or sinking line. The pattern is effective on steelhead and chum salmon on all streams and under all conditions. It is also a very good fly to use in the winter.

6. *Del Cooper* — This steelhead pattern was first introduced by Mike Kennedy of Lake Oswego, Oregon, and named after a noted fly tyer and rod builder from Portland. Tied on sizes #4 and #6, this is a very popular pattern on the Deschutes. It is best fished with a wet-fly swing on a floating line, and is especially effective in low water in bright, sunny weather.

7. *Purple Peril* — Originated by Ken McLeod, a former editor of *The Seattle Times,* this steelhead pattern is widely used on rivers in the Pacific Northwest and British Columbia. It can be tied in sizes #4 and #6, and is best fished with a wet-fly

swing with a floating line. It is a good pattern in clear as well as slightly off-color water.

8. *Tranquilizer* — This pattern was also first introduced by Mike Kennedy. It was originally tied for the 1/2-pound trout found in the Rogue River, but was later popularized for use on steelhead on the North Umpqua by Ed Hartzel, a noted bamboo rod maker from Portland, Oregon. It is a good pattern to use under bright, sunny conditions. It is generally tied in sizes #4 - #8, and is best fished with a wet-fly swing, using a floating line.

9. *McLeod Ugly* — Named for and originated by Ken McLeod, this steelhead pattern was initially tied for Washington and British Columbia streams. It can be tied on sizes #2 - #6, and is fished with a wet-fly swing, using a floating or sinking line. It is effective in high and off-color water.

10. *Greased Liner* — First introduced by Harry Lemire of Black Diamond, Washington, this steelhead pattern was designed for the Wenatchee River in Washington. Tied on sizes #4 and #6, it should be fished as a skater, creating a disturbance on the water's surface. This is an excellent low-water pattern and is most effectively fished with a floating line on the swing. Fishing it with a riffle hitch is equally as effective.

11. *Bucktail Caddis* — This steelhead pattern can be tied in sizes #6 and #8 to simulate an adult caddis. It can be fished with a wet-fly swing on a floating line, or with a slight twitch. The latter method is very effective in October when the large orange-bodied caddis are emerging.

12. *Bucktail Coachman* — This steelhead pattern is an all-purpose attractor. Tied in sizes #4 and #6, it can be fished with a wet-fly swing on a floating or sinking line.

13. *Spruce Fly* — This pattern was first named the Godfrey Special, but was renamed the Spruce Fly, supposedly after the coastal spruce tree. Originally designed for cutthroat trout, this deadly steelhead pattern is tied in sizes #4 - #8. It can be

effectively fished with a wet-fly swing, using a strip or twitch to give it action. Some anglers like to use this pattern with sinking lines in order to simulate baitfish.

14. *Juicy Bug* — First introduced by Ben Chandler and Ike Tower, both of Coos Bay, Oregon, this steelhead pattern is extremely popular on rivers in southern Oregon, including the Rogue and Umpqua. It is a killer on spring/summer steelhead, especially on the Deschutes. Tied in sizes #4 - #8, it can be fished with a wet-fly swing on a floating or sink-tip line. This pattern is a very good waking pattern since its split wings provide pronounced wakes when the fly is twitched.

15. *Orange Comet* — Several tyers from northern California are credited with the development of the various designs of the Comet. Regardless of its originator, it is a deadly pattern when seeking steelhead and coho salmon. Tied in sizes #2 - #6, it is best fished with a wet-fly swing on a sink-tip line. Its design, consisting of a bead head, makes it very effective in deeper water, especially in the winter.

16. *Boss* — Popularized by Grant King of Guerneville, California, who named it after his wife, this pattern was adapted from the Comet series. Like the Comet, it should be fished with a wet-fly swing on a sink-tip line. Tied in sizes #2 - #6, it is a good pattern to use when going after steelhead and chinook salmon, especially in high or off-color water.

17. *Babine Special* — Though this pattern's originator is unknown, it was named after the famed Babine River in British Columbia. Generally tied in sizes #2 - #6, it simulates egg roe and is a good all-weather pattern. It can be fished effectively when going for steelhead, coho, and chinook salmon in all

*Steelhead and Salmon Patterns* — from left to right, top row: *Babine Special, Orange Comet*; 2nd row: *Polar Shrimp, Boss*; 3rd row: *Greased Liner, Thor*; 4th row: *Skykomish Sunrise, Umpqua Special.* ➤

types of water. It is especially good in the winter. The pattern can be fished either with a wet-fly swing or dead drift, using a sinking line.

18. *Polar Shrimp* — Originated on the Eel River in northern California, this pattern is deadly on steelhead, coho, and chinook salmon. Like the Babine Special, it suggests egg roe and should be fished either with a wet-fly swing or dead drift, using a sinking line. Tied in sizes #2 - #6, it is an excellent winter steelhead fly and works well in off-color water.

19. *Skykomish Sunrise* — When Ken and George McLeod designed this fly, it was their intention to capture the image of a sunrise on the Skykomish River in Washington or to "tie a fly that looks like the sky." Tied in sizes #2/0 - #6, this is a versatile all-weather fly, especially popular in British Columbia. It is excellent for use on winter steelhead and coho salmon. Fished with either a wet-fly swing or a dead drift, using a sinking line, this pattern can also be used to simulate eggs.

20. *Umpqua Special* — This famous pattern was developed on the North Umpqua River in Oregon, at Steamboat Springs. Tied in sizes #4 - #6, it should be fished with a wet-fly swing on a sinking line when going for steelhead and pink salmon.

21. *Brad's Brat* — Originated by Enos Bradner, a former editor at *The Seattle Times,* this pattern was developed for use on the Stillaguamish River in Washington. It is a versatile, all-season fly which can be used anywhere in the Pacific Northwest and British Columbia when seeking steelhead and chum salmon. Tied on sizes #2/0 - #6, it can be fished on a wet-fly swing, using either a floating or sinking line.

22. *Thor* — Originated by Jim Pray of Eureka, California, and named after his friend, Walter "Thor" Thoresen, this fly incorporates the colors of the Bucktail Coachman. First fished on the Eel River, it has proven deadly on steelhead and chum salmon. Tied on sizes #1/0 - #6, the pattern should be fished with a wet-fly swing on a sinking line.

23. *Golden Demon* — Also developed by Jim Pray, this steelhead pattern was popularized by Zane Grey on Oregon's Rogue River. Tied in sizes #2 - #6, it should be fished with a wet-fly swing on a floating line. It is very effective in low-water situations.

24. *Fall Favorite* — This pattern was designed by Lloyd Silvius of Eureka, California, who introduced it on the Eel River. It is an excellent pattern to use on steelhead and pink salmon, especially in low-water situations. Tied in sizes #2 - #6, it should be fished with a wet-fly swing, using a floating or sinking line.

OVERLEAF: *Steve Dorn on the Harrison River in British Columbia.*

# A FINAL WORD

When I first started fly fishing back in the 1957, it was with my Dad's bamboo rod and his automatic fly reel. And I confess, I really didn't know exactly what I was doing. I knew nothing about lines or flies or all of the sophisticated presentation techniques that we use today. But, hey, I knew it was fun! At that same time, I was still using hardware tackle with lures, plugs, and live bait. And I enjoyed that type fishing, too. I had a good time and caught lots of fish.

But all of a sudden, the challenge of hardware fishing simply wasn't there for me any more. So in 1969, I became exclusively a fly fisherman. No matter what the weather conditions — high winds, rain, sleet, snow or ice — I was still going to try to go after whatever species of fish I was fishing for with a fly rod.

I begin to realize at that point that the satisfaction in fly fishing was not in the size or numbers of fish I caught, in the sense that I had to prove something to somebody else. Rather, it was from a growing recognition that as my fly-fishing skills increased, my personal satisfaction with the sport increased as well.

It wasn't just being able to find the fish, execute a decent cast and presentation, achieve a successful hook-up, then fight, land, and admire the fish. Added to the considerable satisfaction that the execution of those skills brought me then — and still does today — was the knowledge that I had also gained absolute authority over a great wild fish, and yet had the power, and the will, to release it to swim unharmed and free again in its native water. What a rush! There is simply no sporting chal-lenge in the world to match it.

I hope you will have the chance to come to the Pacific Northwest and join me in the great sport of steelhead and salmon fishing. And if you do, I hope the information I have set forth in this book will be of value to you.

# SELECTED BIBLIOGRAPHY

## BOOKS

Combs, Trey, *Steelhead Fly Fishing* (New York: Lyons & Burford, 1991).

——, *Steelhead Trout* (Portland, Oregon: Frank Amato Publications, 1988).

Fennelly, John F., *Steelhead Paradise* (Portland, Oregon: Frank Amato Publications, 1989).

Meyer, Deke, *Advanced Fly Fishing for Steelhead* (Portland, Oregon: Frank Amato Publications, 1992).

Scott, Jock, *Greased Line Fishing for Salmon* (London: Seely, Service, and Co., Ltd., 1938, 1982).

## VIDEOS

Teeny, Jim, *Catching More Steelhead: Breaking Tradition With Jim Teeny* (St. Paul, Minnesota: Scientific Anglers/3M, 1987).

Waller, Lani, *Advanced Fly Fishing for Pacific Steelhead* (St. Paul, Minnesota: Scientific Anglers/3M, 1987).

——, *Fly Fishing for Pacific Steelhead* (St. Paul, Minnesota: Scientific Anglers/3M, 1987).

# INDEX

## THE TEENY TECHNIQUE
## FOR STEELHEAD AND SALMON

Designed by Robin McDonald, Birmingham, Alabama.

Cover Photograph of the author with a steelhead on the Babine River in British Columbia by Jim Teeny

Color Photography by:
R. Valentine Atkinson/Frontiers (pages 24, 61, 89)
Jim Teeny (pages 2, 8, 12, 19, 25, 46, 50, 55, 58, 63, 67, 70, 108, 123, 128, 150)
Joseph Veras (pages 119, 133, 137, 139, 141, 143, 147)

Illustrated by Rod Walinchus, Livingston, Montana.

Text composed in Berkeley Old Style by Compos-it, Montgomery, Alabama.

Film prepared by Compos-it, Montgomery, Alabama.

Color separations by Photographics, Birmingham, Alabama.

Printed and Bound by Arcata Graphics Company.

Text sheets are acid-free Warren Flo Book by S.D. Warren Company, a division of Scott Paper Company, Boston, Massachusetts.

Endleaves are Rainbow Antique.

Cover cloth is by Holliston, Kingsport, Tennessee.